THE
SWITCHED-ON
CEO

HOW TO THINK LIKE A
WORLD-CLASS LEADER

Steven R. Falk, M.A.

ADVANCE PRAISE *Switched-On CEO*

The one book on effective leadership I'd have if I could have just one. A landmark book.

—Jordan Nicolussi, President, Sibola Mountain Falling Ltd

Switchback has not only taught me how to stay in the proper headspace, but has given me the tools to teach my kids. Steven Falk has done an outstanding job developing such a useful set of tools.

—Troy Young, General Manager, Roga Contracting Ltd., REHN Enterprises Ltd.

Steven displays great insight into how we think and why. I believe this book will change my life and many others for the better.

B. David Ashcroft, Industrial Manager

Most employers are not consciously aware they have a problem until the situation gets so bad they are actively looking for a resolve. *Switched-On CEO: How to Think Like a World-Class Leader* describes the Switchback technique; it allows individual permission to have feelings, empathy and compassion. I have witnessed how the Switchback process works, and I envision people applying the techniques of Switchback in all parts of their lives to deal with our respond to situations where conflicting personalities are present.

Rob Gill, Maintenance Operations Manager

The *Switched-On CEO* contains critically needed information and strategy for the healthcare leaders of today. Steven Falk brings remarkable clarity to the causes and perpetuating factors that underlay sub-optimal workplace culture which often hinder quality, patient care and wear down employees. He then provides practical and proven methods to transform a dysfunctional staff environment into a highly effective and cooperative team.

Caleb DePutter, MD

"*The Switched-On CEO* showed me that people can change, brain science proves it, and change can be achieved in days rather than years. I'm excited to apply Steve's world-class thinking and Switched-On Leadership skills in my world of wealth coaching and behavioural economics, to help my business clients better leverage their greatest assets, their teams. Switchback's wealth of experience, systems and tools gives me great confidence.

Curtis Scoville, Wealth Coach, Life Insurance Advisor,
And CEO of Scoville & Associates Inc.

Editor: Karen Rowe, www.karenrowe.com
Cover Design: Shake Creative, ShakeTampa.com
Inside Layout: Ljiljana Pavkov
Interior Graphics: © 2018 Switchback Systems Corp.

Printed in the United States

ISBN: 978-1-7752813-0-6 (international trade paper edition)
ISBN: 978-1-7752813-1-3 (ebook)

To Karen Falk,

For taking the big leap in 1985 and saying yes to marrying me.

A journey of: family, entrepreneurial adventure, risk and reward.

Table of Contents

THE
SWITCHED-ON
CEO

Introduction

CONGRATULATIONS ON REACHING THE LEVEL OF
CEO. That is a big achievement in itself, but it's one that
comes with unique challenges.

When I'm invited into a CEO's office, I usually meet
a really nice person who is overworked, in desperate
need of real, honest relationships, and is troubled by
self-doubts. The position is a tough one to fill, and some
days it can feel like death by a thousand cuts.

One of the problems is the position itself. You're
the leader of the company, so who is going to give you
honest feedback and support? Who can you trust? Your
subordinates aren't going to give you honest feedback.
The board of directors may be too caught up in their
own world to call you on things when they should.
Your wife or husband may have stopped talking to
you at this level of honesty years ago. Are your kids
in a position of power to call you on things? Your
brother? Your sister? Have they any idea the kind of

pressure you live under? How could they? They're not in your shoes.

This situation may sound rather doomsday. In truth, 90% of your life is most likely put together, successful, and ticking along. But that remaining 10% may be sabotaging the 90% of your life that is going well. What if you could master that last 10%?

Throughout this book, I invite you to take a private look at what may be holding you back from mastery. The whole process could be internal and not even seen by your peers or your family. At Switchback, we have the thinking and tools to reveal, understand, manage, shift and transform the 10% that is holding you and your organization back from world class success.

But first, let's start at the beginning.

How did you get here, in the first place?

Let's say you became CEO just before you hit 40, and you were on top of the world. You were ready for it: everything you'd been doing prepared you for this moment. You were the boss, the one in charge, and you wanted the responsibility. You knew you were a leader. You were ready to innovate; long before disruption theory was popular you were ready to disrupt. You were ready to win at all costs and go to war with your troops. It didn't intimidate you at all in one part of your brain, yet another part of your brain was terrified.

Over time, things changed. Reality set in. Your team – stretched over multiple departments – stopped having your back. Meetings were functional at best. You didn't know if your assistant was married or not, and you didn't really care. Drama infiltrated every department, and you battled against so many currents each day that when the big battle came, you had nothing left.

More and more you would come home late; a 65-hour workweek became the norm. Your family? Who are they? Policies, procedures, bureaucracy, insurance, legality all the big stuff came down – hard – on your shoulders. Your brain was getting to the edge of its capacity to manage stress. You unconsciously started to withdraw from the team at work, and from the team at home. You knew in theory you could run a successful company, but in reality, it was falling apart.

Your brain is telling you that you need to process the stress, not just store and absorb it; it is telling you that you need to reach out to trustworthy team members, but you have closed the door in your office and are blankly staring at your mountain of work. Just shake it off and lead, you tell yourself. But it's not quite that simple.

As CEO, you were hired to have a voice. Originally, you had a voice. Over time, however, you've risk-managed your voice right out of your throat and even right out of your life. You can't even stand in front of your senior management and speak off-script and if you do it comes out sounding either passive or aggressive. You've lost faith in the concept of team.

LOSING FAITH IN TEAM

PASSIVE   TEAM   AGGRESSIVE

This type of passive aggression is not world-class. Meanwhile, on the front lines people are putting their life and limb in danger. They're living in a culture that is being mirrored by your leadership. In some industries, you can actually measure the lack of leadership by fatalities. In most, it is just measured through the dreary metrics that hang around your neck.

Bottom line: Someone's got to have the courage to walk into your office with the great decor, a sofa and the mountain of work and lend a hand. But you have to invite that someone in.

Switchback offers the opportunity for CEOs to gain honest feedback in private. Each chapter of this book peels off another layer of self-awareness, situational awareness and self-reflection so you can look deeply into your life. You have a tremendous opportunity to influence and a tremendous opportunity to inspire. Yet, I rarely come across a CEO who still has gas in the tank to do either of these tasks well.

Switchback has tools to help you transform your life and revitalize your organization. But for us to help, we need your invitation. To do that you need to trust us. Think of this book as our humble offering of trust so that we can help you become what I call a Switched-On CEO.

A New Paradigm of Leadership Training

Ideas and information are not enough, it's the implementation of ideas that changes the world. Our company, Switchback Systems Corp, has set itself apart from information products by delivering on the implementation of ideas. Employees from all walks of life come to us after a three-day Switchback training and passionately ask, "How can I get my CEO to understand how powerful Switchback training is? We need this throughout our whole company. We need it now."

As CEO, imagine a future where you catch yourself driving home from the office on Friday afternoon, humming a song and knowing your brain is in a sweet spot with a quarter tank of brain power still in reserve for your weekend.

Interested?

If I told you I know a proven way to shift your company culture to achieve this outcome in record time, would that pique your interest?

How about witnessing the 180 degree turnaround of your most difficult employee is just 3 days? We do this consistently.

We stepped into a situation where a company had an average of forty union grievances per year from a union crew of under 100 – a serious culture issue – and helped them reduce their average annual grievances down to four. And we did that in less than a year.

It is generally thought that creating a shift in workplace culture takes seven to eight years without outside help, and three to four years with industry-standard training. What if I told you that at Switchback, we have developed a way for you to accomplish this same culture shift within just 12 months?

We make it simple and easy. With over 40 diagrams supporting Switchback's strategy and true-life examples backing up our global impact, we offer a custom-designed playbook for you and your company's success.

Imagine a Monday morning at your organization's headquarters. Your staff are genuinely interested in each other's lives. They understand the importance of connecting after their weekend and strategizing for the day and week ahead. This is not happening by chance. This is what we at Switchback call the implementation of a Switched-On culture, organized and engaged.

This is an intentional cultural core value. It's like a perfect pairing: wine and cheese, pearls and black dress, peanut butter and jelly. People and productivity go hand in hand, not one or the other. It's what a Switched-On organization looks like, and the dream for just about any CEO.

There are absolutely critical moments in your role as a CEO when you need to be Switched-On. I see it like having the capacity, wisdom and strength to walk through the front door of a critical situation and be a leader. There are some front doors that are very tough to walk through, but you're the one who has to do it.

When tragedy strikes your phone will ring no matter where you are no matter what you are doing. As the CEO, you have to be able to walk through the front door of the family that just lost their son in a work place accident and connect deeply for 45 minutes. Other people, like the Switchback team, have the task of entering that same door later to support the process and to sit with the family until they can muster up the strength to build a long-term plan around their loss. A Switched-On CEO works with the team to serve the situation with world class compassion. Your ability to walk through that "door" and deliver results will set your company culture apart.

When you don't walk through the front door at that critical moment of need, guess who else doesn't walk through? VPs don't walk through. Managers don't walk through. Supervisors don't walk through. When you do, you model leadership to all who are watching.

Developing a Switched-On CEO is only one part of our company's overarching strategic plan to help CEOs of large companies and government departments deliver solid, measurable results in record time. How? By leveraging your greatest asset: your culture.

People are fascinating. If you can catch their interest – which is both harder and easier than you may think – you can achieve rapid culture change. We have designed everything we do in a way that builds high levels of engagement with not just the early adopters but with the most resistant, difficult employees. Employees run home to teach their families and integrate Switchback into their daily lives. This is one of our secret keys that speeds up cultural transformation ten-fold.

A Switched-On TEAM

The Switchback definition of TEAM is Quadrant 2 in our four-quadrant diagram, which I'll explain in a moment. It's, front of the brain, organized and engaged. Switchback Systems Corp is a movement of innovative, nimble-thinking experts who deliver results through a firm and friendly, mentally tough, logical and powerful system of thinking that is making a huge difference in corporate culture. A measure of our success with some of our clients is the actual reduction of industrial fatalities. We are on a mission.

Our battle cry:

People can change

The power of success is in team

Often the cost of the journey to the top is that you become an expert at shuffling around the needs of others. You become an expert at shifting your priorities toward the priorities of your Board of Directors, your stakeholders, your shareholders, your executive team and all their quirks.

There's a missing piece. If you want to be a world-class leader, when people look in your eyes, they have to see life. When people hear your voice, they have to hear life. When they feel your handshake, they have to feel life. This is only possible if you are as committed to your own journey of achievement and transformation as you are committed to the success of the people in the world around you.

You can build around you a culture of world class TEAM. TEAM with government regulators, environmentalists, your Board of Directors right down to the newest young worker. TEAM at home and in the community.

The journey to building TEAM is about understanding your thoughts, managing your memories and setting your goals on targets that you can self-regulate in the moment, daily, and monthly with yourself and your team. The key is mental toughness or, as our title states, being Switched-On.

If you want to be a world-class leader and build world-class teams, we have a playbook that's going to switch your brain on and give you clearly defined targets based on diagrams that will meet your needs, as well as the needs of your complex and varied team commitments.

In Part One I'll reveal my story with you, tell you how Switchback was created, and give you an overview of Switchback's theory:

• The core principle that People Can Change
• Switchback's 4 Quadrants diagram and how to use this tool to analyze teams

- How our brains store memories
- How a part of our brain stores what I call memory X's
- The importance of moving memory X's

You'll also learn about why I feel so passionate about this work.

Part Two is grounded in our belief that the Power of Success is in TEAM. You'll learn a terrific communication tool we call the 3-Lane Highway, and how to apply it. We'll take a look at the six Profiles that make up our reactive thinking and behaviors and how they might show up in your team. Finally, you will get to read about how to put Switchback thinking to work.

After being a Family Therapist in private practice for over two decades and a business consultant for ten years, I have learned that mental toughness and building healthy functional relationships are at the core of leadership. Your organization is like a complex extended family. It all starts with you, the CEO.

PART 1

Switchback System Thinking Revealed

Chapter 1

The Good Old Days Are Gone

IN WHAT WE REFER TO AS THE "GOOD OLD DAYS," the CEO was chosen the way a pack of dogs chooses its leader. The hiring committee looked for the meanest, gruffest, toughest, hardest-working, maybe alcoholic, barrel-chested white male, the biggest head they could find in the room, and pointed at him and said, "I think you'll make a great boss."

Why? Because that guy could swear like a sailor and scare people. As it turns out, that's how we were parenting back then, too. Don't get me wrong: most parents were loving and kind, but they still used some of the same leadership tools that the corporate world was using. It was a simplistic model of leadership known as "fear and intimidation." People responded to it, but it didn't build a sustainable culture of trust. It created loyalty, but not the kind of loyalty a company culture wants; it's like the loyalty of a dog that emits a little squirt of pee when it comes to you.

Whether it was a football coach or a CEO, that used to be the model of leadership. In some spheres that model still exists because old cultures sometimes take forever to die. There are still NFL coaches who work within this old school model. They use fear and intimidation and the threat of withdrawal of relationship to gain loyalty: I won't talk to you, I'll bench you, and then you'll work hard for me. The motivation was based on negativity, and while that style can be really effective in the short term, it is also really damaging.

Amazingly, leadership paradigms shifted through the 1970s, which was a major push back from "old school methods." I was public schooled for half my childhood within the 70's model and, believe me, it wasn't sustainable either. That leadership model was all about rejecting the old and inventing unproven, unsuccessful theories around leadership and team. Any time society shifts due to a reaction to an old model we get a pendulum swing but not necessarily a new world-class paradigm. The 70's battle cry in my small west coast community educational system was "all you need is love, structure is bad." This was a fun environment to hang out in but didn't help us kids learn how to sound out words or gain reading and writing skills.

Throughout these cultural swings brain science and systems thinking gradually gained a voice, and so here we are.

Think about our commitment to brain rehabilitation today, compared to the "good old days." The way we rehabilitate brain injuries now has completely evolved from the tentative efforts in the past.

The world we live in today is entirely different. We used to think the brain was logical and sequential and relatively static. We also thought personalities were relatively static. Now we know it's not true: the brain actually can adapt. We can leverage the same understanding within organizations.

I was once an expert witness in a court case and the judge asked this question: "Can people change their personalities?" I stopped, took a breath, perceived that she was laying a trap, thought about my response and said, "Your honor, the real question is, can people choose to be functional or dysfunctional within their unique personality?" Later, on the court house steps, the lawyers from both sides congratulated me on my answer. Apparently, this was a trap that the judge had used before to try to discredit expert witnesses by getting them to insist that people can change their personalities. I still think it's all about being functional and healthy and that personality is not the biggest factor affecting success.

I believe our brains can find new pathways to achieve new results within our personalities. Current brain science is also really disruptive to outdated personality testing. The classic personality test, Myers-Briggs, steered people towards having to commit to one of 16 personality types. This scripting has always made me very uncomfortable. I have witnessed over the years that personality testing exercises generally push people out of teams rather than building teams.

Today, we have a real hybrid. We have a culture that doesn't know what to do with leaders. Old school? 1970s? Personality types? It's hard to pick a target and aim for something if we can't agree what world class looks like.

Switchback says we don't actually care whether your background is old school or 1970s, or what your personality type is. What we care about is whether you're functional and healthy, and whether people are drawn to you or repelled by you. Do you have the skill and style to build and sustain a team?

When I built out the model and theory for Switchback, I wasn't actually taking personality into consideration. I was taking functionality and health into consideration. I believe a functional leader is a leader who has their act together; they're organized, and they have the capacity to connect with people. I don't care if they connect with a booming voice, I don't care if they connect with a really sweet soft voice, I don't care if it's a touch on the shoulder or a high five. What I care about is if they have the ability to connect and be organized and, beyond that, have the ability to read their audience and know what's appropriate to achieve connection and structure.

As the world becomes more global, we're going to be confronted with even more leadership paradigms. I have taken tours of Asia and Australasia, Africa, and Europe, and observed that there are clearly many different ways to communicate within organizational systems. When we tested out our Switchback model in Mongolia while working with financial regulators, and in Malawi, Africa with NGOs, what we discovered was fascinating. Although they each had a completely different leadership paradigm, every one of our diagrams was spot on as a relevant application for each entity.

The changing world is going to need models that are robust without being ethno-centric or gender-centric; models that define leadership not by culture or personality but by striving for foundational targets that directly impact the human experience in the workplace. This has always been our intention at Switchback: to build a timeless, tested model that works beyond borders.

Just as parenting has evolved and gone through its cycles, leadership is undergoing its own evolution at the corporate level. Not only that, the whole system is constantly changing and growing; we have twenty-something computer programmers suddenly tasked with leading multi-billion-dollar tech companies they've started. In a world that is constantly changing, what is the one thing that seems to remain? Our need to connect, our need to stay organized. Our need to lead effectively – and our need to be led effectively.

It's time to embrace a new way of leading, a way that keeps the leader's brain Switched-On and the team fully engaged. We call it Switchback, and every time we train a new company in this framework, we see tremendous results.

Chapter 2

The Switchback Background

I ALMOST DIED WHEN I WAS TWO.

I grew up in a small farming community called Black Creek, on Vancouver Island. When I was two, there was a meningitis outbreak so severe that a couple of kids died from it. My dad had just given up his teaching job and sold the house. We were moving to Winnipeg, where my parents would become college students with the goal of becoming Christian missionaries.

I was the fourth child, and there I was, sick and dying. As my parents drove me to the hospital in Comox, I lay in my mother's arms, completely paralyzed. My mother and father cried out to God. Like many parents in desperate moments, they surrendered my life to God thinking that I was about to die.

There is a story in the bible about Isaac, the son of Abraham, being offered on the altar, and here it was again, playing out on Vancouver Island. They gave me to God. They said to God, "We don't know what you're doing, but you can have Steve 100%. We give him to you."

As we arrived at the community Catholic hospital, the nuns gathered to offer their care to my parents. When the doctor began his examination, he tested the paralysis by trying to bend my neck. In that moment I was healed. It was not the work of the doctor or any medical treatment administered, but something supernatural. My mom and dad say that the air became like gelatin. They felt they could've floated at that moment, had they wanted to.

With the nuns in awe, the doctor finished his exam and announced, "Well I guess you've got your Steven back." They drove home, their sick child now completely healed.

There is a possibility that they didn't get their child back fully, because after that I was a little different. I developed a radically different relationship with my intuition, and an ability to sense the essence of others; at least, I could tell whether they were good or bad. I also was tormented by night visions and, as I grew older I found basic scholastic achievement very difficult.

My parents witnessed these complexities in me and tried a whole variety of interventions to try to keep me "switched-on": A puppy, a gun, youth sports, grandpa's woodwork shop, one-on-one time – all noble attempts to help out their kid. Looking back, I could have really used Switchback thinking and tools.

A Switched-On Leader

If I could give you the clear picture in a paragraph of how I came to be attending graduate school, I would. It was the result of a long and far-from-ordinary chain of events. It was a mystery to everyone – myself included – how I came to be attending graduate school at all, not to mention in a psychology program to become a marriage and family therapist.

Two weeks into grad school, I was called into the Head of the Psychology Department's office. He sat behind his desk in an office full of books, his bald head glowing like a big egg. I sat down across from him in a worn-out antique chair, below his eye level. It felt like I was 11 years old again, back in the principal's office with all the old symptoms, heart racing, shallow breath, sweating, losing focus and concentration.

He asked me seriously, "Steve, how did you get through our screening program?"

Stupid question, I thought to myself. Why are you asking me?

"Seriously. Some of the material you're handing in is not really graduate level," he told me.

Ah, you're a genius. How did you figure that out? You're the first one that's ever diagnosed me as a gifted, talented under-achiever. Well done. So went my inner thoughts.

I didn't say anything, however, because I had borrowed money from my grandma in order to attend school, and I had a new-born baby in tow. The risk of failure was huge – and I couldn't head back to Canada as a failure.

The department head got up, and what he did next really struck me. To this day, this memory reminds me of the power of leadership.

He walked over to the blinds and opened them. "Steve, come over here," he summoned me beside him to the window. *He's a psychologist*, I thought. *Anything could be a metaphor.*

He looked out the window and said, "Do you see all those ramps? A couple of years ago we had a student join us who was in a wheelchair. He stated his desire to come to our school and gave us a notice of one year. During that year, we ramped the whole campus for him. Of course, the classy thing would have been for us to have ramps in place before his request, because it would have been the right thing to do." (This took place before regulations around accessibility had been established).

The Department Head told me, "We ramped the whole campus for him." Then he looked at me with eyes that said, *Are you going to fight me or are you going to join my team?*

After a few moments, he continued, "If you're interested, we can ramp the campus for you."

We can ramp the campus for you! It was a transformational statement that changed my brain and my life forever.

"Here's the deal," he continued. "Never hand in another hand-written assignment to anybody in any course for the remainder of your years here."

I said, "Okay."

He said, "Do as much as you can at home where you can stay calm and produce. There's a university right next door. Get someone to help you – maybe your wife can help you. Don't write any exams in class. Just go home. Calm down. We're interested in your brain – in your gifted thinking. The other stuff is rudimentary. But we have to be able to read it."

The question is, how loyal did I become and how hard did I work for that leader? I put in 65+ hours a week for him. I laughed and cried my way through graduate school. As I faced my pain and weaknesses I produced sometimes brilliant work. It was amazing. Thanks to that singled five-minute conversation, my entire life changed. I ended up being one of the school valedictorians and this amazing department head's assistant. I am forever thankful to that man.

I was his teaching assistant (which is very prestigious position in graduate school), and he tailored my duties to match my gifts and abilities. Instead of doing research or indexes, I helped run his communication labs. There was no written reporting. I would run the group sessions and then sit in his office to verbally debrief, sharing every micro observation I made.

Switchback is communication labs. I've taken that experience from graduate school all those years ago and transported it into industry. A participant can read at a grade 4 level in our program, and be a rock star. No one would know what difficulties the participant is wrestling with, and he or she would never be exposed or humiliated.

Many leaders have no idea the power and influence they have over people's lives. But if you look for the gold (giftedness, skills and abilities) in people and try to provide ways to help them be successful, you can make a huge difference for them. Why not treat people this way?

I learned a few years later one of the reasons that department head had been so compassionate. His own son had a brain very similar to mine, and his son's journey through high school was breaking his dad's heart. That could have been one of the deeper reasons why he took interest, mined the gold and built TEAM with me.

When the Red Phone Rang

Partially due to the tremendous impression that man had on my life and my work, I became a successful family therapist. My experience working with him as my leader

33

probably set the stage for my own ability to work with the outliers and the gifted and talented underachievers.

My career flourished and, as our children grew up, I began coaching minor hockey. I didn't qualify to be a high-end rep coach, so there I was, among eight other coaches picking our team for the local "house" hockey league. The other coaches would say things like, "This kid has huge violence issues, so he's on your team," or, "This girl doesn't know how to skate, she's been picked on all her life – she's on your team." And I took them. I took them all, happily. It was my beautiful outlier "Mighty Ducks" team, and it was great. We got soundly beaten in every game at the start of the season, but by the end of the season we had built world class TEAM. We leveraged TEAM and average-at-best technical hockey knowledge and managed to win our share of games in the end-of-season tournament. TEAM delivered measurable results, not just a "good feeling."

It's funny how small victories are as much transformational as are actual achievements. At one small out-of-town tournament, our humble team ended up battling to the finals and winning. The prize, to our surprise, was a three-foot-tall trophy. The way the kids skated around with this big, shiny trophy at the end of the game was a memory for the ages.

I was just in our attic and there it was: the huge trophy. I brought it down and found it a new home in the bedroom two of our grandsons use. There it stands in all its glory. My efforts as a coach that year were recognized by the whole league with the award of coach of the year.

I never would have thought my connection to minor hockey – or even my aptitude to build TEAM with these kids – would have led to professional success, yet, in a roundabout way, it did. One year, the director of safety of one of the largest employers in the community had a rebellious 14-year-old boy who should have made the rep team but didn't because of his attitude. He had been demoted to the house hockey league, and guess whose team he was put on? There is a very small window of time to win over a young man who has been shamed and demoted and assigned to a new team. I needed to leverage every theoretical modality that I possessed to win his trust and loyalty within hours and days, not weeks, months or years. While I was working my strategic culture shifting plan with all the kids, that boy's dad was in the stands watching every move and wondering, *Who is this guy? What's the magic?*

Several years later the "red phone" rang – you know, the call right out of the blue that changes your life. Jokingly, and actually very seriously, our family, pays close attention to the "red phone."

This call was especially interesting: it was from the hockey dad, now a director of safety. There had been a serious accident involving a hand faller (the person who cuts down trees) in his company. The senior leaders were struggling to find someone to help them understand what went wrong and how they could mitigate the issue moving forward. The director of safety knew me as his kid's hockey coach, and that I had been working both as a family therapist and a human factor industrial consultant. He took a chance on me, betting on the theory that an expert in systems thinking would be able to translate family systems thinking into industrial safety culture thinking. Know this, people are watching, they are watching to see if we are who we say we are (integrity). They are also watching, searching for inspiration and innovation.

This was at a time when, tragically, workers in the logging industry was still losing their lives at a very unacceptable rate. The Work Safe folks were working overtime to try to curb the crisis with new rules and regulations while the newly formed Forest Safety Council was adding to the effort with certifications and audits. The missing piece, however, was the human factor: culture.

When I first arrived in the board room with the director of safety and his colleagues, they sat me down and went over every detail of the event for over an hour. Then they asked me a simple question. "What do you see that we don't see?" It was the perfect transformational moment. Everything I'd been diagramming for 22 years in my small, private office led to this moment.

You may know the 10,000-hour rule: that we excel at whatever we have spent 10,000 hours doing. At this point I had done more than 10,000+ hours of diagramming complex family systems in often hostile, high stakes therapy sessions. Family systems theory teaches that individual reactions and responses correlate with stimuli we get from our systems, and particularly from our family of origin. This was the moment to put my family systems expertise to work.

The tree was dead. It was just a snag, and the faller's only job was to get it down safely. The faller was on the company's safety committee; he had 15 years' experience, and a beautiful family. There was no reason for him to break the rules and regulations, to disregard his certification and his expertise built on more than 10,000 hours. Why then did he? What happened in his brain?

On that day, the logger's chain saw got stuck while he was cutting on the back side of the tree because the tree leaned back on the cutting bar. It happens from time to time, and this time it triggered an adrenaline rush, which sent the faller to the back of his brain triggering an intense fight-or-flight response. His first thought, likely, was in the flight response, as he probably wondered if he'd been seen making a mistake. There was another group working on the other side of the hill, and potentially still others watching him work. He may have thought everybody saw him do it, which is an exaggeration but nonetheless would have kicked the back part of his brain into gear, causing him to pull as hard as he could on his saw to free it and get himself out of the upsetting condition.

It didn't work. He couldn't pull it out, so then his brain ramped up the flight-or-fight response. Now his brain was starting to give him irrational ways to solve his problem. As a result, he started to use the back of his axe to pound tree wedges in the back cut on the tree. In this situation he was breaking the rules. You're only supposed to do this on solid trees, not dead trees.

By now his heart was racing: body was sweating, breath was shallow, vision was tunneling and his ability to think straight was rapidly disappearing. The irrational part of his brain was yelling at him, "Get the tree down at all costs." His back brain was in rebellion to what he knew was right. It was also close to the end of the day, so other factors like fatigue and lowered blood sugar had begun to affect his concentration and focus.

Then it happened. Without warning, the tree came down on top of him and nearly killed him. During the investigation, no one could figure out how this expert could have done this. He was certified by the Forest Council, he was on the safety committee, and upper management was confounded as to how they could help him and equally importantly keep this from happening to someone else.

The answer lay in the inner thinking of his brain. This hand faller didn't recognize as dangerous the triggers that he was experiencing in his brain and body. He was losing access to his rational front brain each time he gave into the flight-or-fight response, until he was probably using 90% of his back brain and only 10% of his front brain. The 10% was clearly telling him to stop but it was drowned out by all the back of the brain stimulus and chatter.

With profuse sweating and tunnel vision, he wasn't seeing anything clearly anymore and the pervading thought was most likely, "something must die, fight to the death." This is a very common danger reaction, whether you're cutting down a tree, checking your emails or being challenged in a meeting. If you receive an email written in all caps from someone who is important to you, adrenaline can start pumping and you can be instantly in a very upset condition so you're not thinking straight. If someone challenges your competence in a meeting, things can unravel fast in your brain.

Because of my healing experience at two years old, my grad school transformation, and my years of really working hard to help people sort out their complex chal- lenges – and the fact that I was responding to a "red phone" summons – I knew this moment in the meeting was special. Still, as I started walking out after the meet- ing, I was surprised when the safety director called my name and physically pinned me against the wall in the hallway. "You have no idea what happened in there do you?" he said with very intense eyes.

I shook my head.

"You just blew us away," he continued. The room had in fact blown up when I drew out the Switchback diagram of the brain, showing clearly the 14 flight-or-fight thoughts that drove the faller out of rational thinking and into tragically irrational thinking.

"You're going to go home and tell your wife that your life as you know it is over. You're building this up into a training. We'll be your first client. You'll develop it with us, right here, and when you're ready, you'll give it to the world. This will save lives."

So that's just what I did. And here I am now, giving it to the world. Giving it to you.

Chapter 3

The Switchback Basics

WHEN THE SAFETY DIRECTOR PINNED ME AGAINST the wall and told me to develop the flight-or-fight diagram into a training, I saw that this was the turn of the season in my career. After 22 years, I hadn't stopped enjoying being a family therapist, but I knew that the season had come to an end. With a clear conscience, in one easy move, my wife and I shifted all our resources, time, and focus into what's now known as Switchback Systems Corp.

I was like all courageous, positive, glass half-full, silver lining entrepreneurs. I built out a ten-year plan for Switchback that would develop a team of itinerant trainers who covered territories and had won the favor and trust of industry and government leaders. It was an ambitious plan, but I am a big believer in aiming as high as you can when you set a target.

It wasn't until a CEO steamrolled my oldest brother (who had joined Switchback), and me over dinner that we really made the shift we needed to spur our business on. He pointed out that we were focused on the workers and their supervisors and were totally neglecting the CEOs. With passion in his voice he shouted at us in the restaurant, "If you don't develop the vision and capacity to help the CEOs, you will never fulfill the calling and destiny of Switchback." We got it.

We took the words of that CEO at face value and instantly shifted our mindset. As a result, we have completed a number of multi-year contracts with government and large businesses, becoming friends with CEOs. The ten-year plan holds true to what we originally saw in our minds, and we are growing this company to its fullest capacity. We're building beautiful teams. We are aligned with leaders who can help Switchback reach within government and large industry. We are witnessing the culture needle move.

This book carries incredible lessons on engaging your team, building out systems, and understanding the complexity of communication, all of which you can apply as CEO. You have two choices: You can learn in real time when faced with a difficult situation. Or you can sit in the privacy of your office with this book open, contemplating what you need to learn before you are faced with a difficult situation. We recommend the latter choice.

The Fundamentals

The fundamentals of Switchback are these beliefs: People can change, and the power of success is in team.

The hard skills and techniques to learn, that stack on top of these beliefs, represent your journey of achievement. The soft skills include shifting beliefs, and they represent your journey of transformation.

With Switchback, I have taken the best of Family Systems Theory, ideas that I had been developing for over two decades, and transformed it into the Switchback System. Witnessing Switchback Systems transform lives and organizations has been a journey that I hope never ends.

We at Switchback believe people can change, that true, sustainable success is found in the power of team, and that teams are built by great leaders. We also know that leaders need to continue to change, grow and transform in order to remain world class.

The Switchback System leads you through the process of understanding how our stored memories form our core values, and how our core values direct our thoughts which ultimately produce the actions by which we are judged.

Workplace Culture

Never underestimate the power of leadership when it comes to transforming workplace culture. Culture is created by people, and established by leaders. I know some people say culture is what happens when the leader is not present, but from what I've seen everyone is actually watching for clues from the leader as to what is important. Whether it is children watching their parents at home or employees keeping an eye on the C-suite, people are watching their leader's micro-responses to stimuli.

Determining and acting upon the company's core values contributes to establishing company culture. "People are our greatest asset", is often quoted as a core value of companies, and I couldn't agree more that this statement is true. However, it is rare that I see it carried out in practice. Instead, CEOs focus their attention first on compliance to rules and regulations, and second on systems that will help the company stay within the compliance standards.

It is natural to lean on rules, regulations, and systems when challenges arise with competitors, market share, costs, profits, and changing market conditions. The human factor is complex and seemingly unreliable, so it is often under-leveraged. However let's put these factors into return on investment (ROI) terms.

Compare the same investment in rules, regulations, and systems with an equal investment in the human factor. The first might yield a 2-4% return, while the second could yield 12-20%! It makes really good business sense to go after the low-hanging fruit, the human factor, for overall metric improvement. The Switchback system is a tool that can get the most out of your organization's human capital.

SETTING THE TARGET

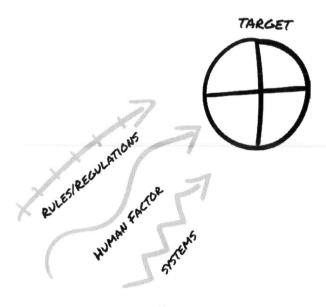

Often when CEOs and their leadership teams have a conversation around the Target Diagram above, they self-identify their lack of focus on the human factor. Over the course of our three-day program, they often come back to this diagram when they are looking for innovative responses to chronic company issues. "There it is again," they say. "We are in love with our systems and not leveraging our human capital."

A similar scenario plays out when CEOs review what Switchback calls the Quadrant System.

The Quadrant System

As a family therapist, I learned that no two families are the same. I especially liked seeing what kind of car the family arrived in for their first appointment. This was an early micro-clue that Switched-On family therapists can't avoid. The super clean, not necessarily new, well maintained two-seater vehicle told me a story. The un-maintained, dirty truck full of last year's receipts and drive-through garbage told a story. The late model seven-passenger minivan with bald tires and stickers all over it told a story. The new four-door truck with the six-cylinder engine told a story. The vehicles gave strong indications of what the people who pulled up in these cars would be like, in terms of their values, thinking, behaviors, and choices.

I wanted to capture families' stories and to plot them to help both me and my clients. Specifically, I wanted to:

• Externalize their reality
• Help them to gain an outside understanding of their lives

- Help them find the epiphany, the seed to lasting transformational change
- Capture the process on paper in one dimension
- Execute the plan using diagrams
- Manage and monitor the journey with diagrams
- Build in long-term continuity with diagrams

I began developing a system and diagrams to put my ideas into theory. I considered the criteria I wanted to meet when I came up with systems or diagrams. Among these were:

- Micro to Macro application (applicable on both the interpersonal and international levels)
- Works in the moment and over long time periods, so the diagram reflects both a moment that passes in a second and longer events (like the rise and fall of a nation)
- Gender inclusive
- Age inclusive
- Culturally inclusive
- Socio-economically inclusive
- Stands the test of time
- Draws on common sense from theological, anthropological, sociological and psychological perspectives
- Is understandable, explainable and applicable for both an under-educated worker and someone with a seat in the corporate boardroom
- Simple and profound (not one or the other)
- Memorable
- Able to demonstrate movement and change, non-static

- Able to describe the problem and demonstrate the solution (not one or the other)
- Is demonstrably defensible intellectual property

I worked with these criteria, keeping in mind my goals, and designed the Quadrant System.

THE FOUR QUADRANTS

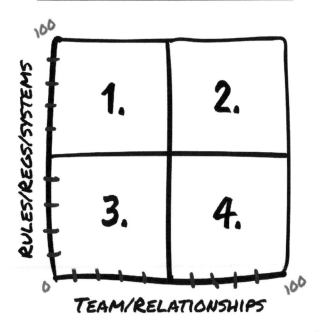

The Quadrant system begins with an X/Y axis, where the Y axis represents rules / regulations / systems / policies, and the X axis represents relationships / team / communication.

Quadrant 1

Quadrant 1 is at the top left. People in this quadrant are high on rules, systems, structures, policies and procedures. They are low in communication, relationships, team-building and camaraderie. They solve problems by producing more rules, regulations, or systems, and their greatest fear moving from Quadrant 1 to Quadrant 2 is their perceived loss of control. That super-clean two-seater that pulled up for a session was driven by someone in Quadrant 1; they love their car, but they're not so in love with people.

Quadrant 1 folks tend to have a favorite saying: "If you want it done right, do it yourself." It should be no surprise that this thinking pushes people to metrics-driven roles, like accounting and finance. They also often over-compensate on the rules and regulations to hide a lack of social skills and comfort in group settings.

Understandably, a lot of CEOs come from engineering, finance, and technical backgrounds. If you're a Quadrant 1 CEO, you may even be a first born or only child, and never had to negotiate or fight for things or people's attention. Your world was self-determined, orderly, controlled and achievement-based.

As you advanced in your career you were able to lean on your Y axis skill set. Producing results with "things" was the way to get noticed. Now, as CEO, your role has expanded to Quadrant 2, and all those social skills that you observed from a distance – and even internally put down as useless, like the socially-comfortable sales folks who seem to effortlessly endear themselves to anyone and everyone in the office – are needed.

These people skills are required to build up the trust and culture of the company and it is the CEO's job to lead by example. Closing the door on this opportunity and busying yourself with all the things that need doing comes at the cost of developing a world-class culture. It also leads to manifesting the Quadrant 1 CEO's greatest fear, which is losing control. Giving into this fear results in micro-managing, or sticking with the old adage that if you want something done right, you have to do it yourself.

Quadrant 4

Directly opposite Quadrant 1, in the lower right square, is Quadrant 4. People in Quadrant 4 have high people skills, team spirit, communication, and camaraderie. They are low on rules, systems, structures, policies and procedures. They solve problems by leveraging their relationships, having more fun and throwing more parties.

For Quadrant 4 folks, their greatest fear around moving from Quadrant 4 to Quadrant 2 is the perceived loss of freedom. Their favorite activity is anything fun, spontaneous, new; and their least favorite activities are paperwork, systems-related work, or processes that trim back their freedom. People in Quadrant 4 gravitate to outside sales or become owner-operators, and often they are hiding Y-axis limitations, like poor spelling or difficulty with technical reading and writing. In terms of the car in my parking lot, the Quadrant 4 person was driving the minivan with the bald tires and stickers all over it. They love their family, but this love is not reflected in basic car maintenance.

As a Quadrant 4 CEO you most likely came up through marketing, sales or communications, and have gained the corner office by winning friends and influencing people. You might even be a fourth-born child like myself and had to charm and negotiate your way into your older siblings' favor. You were never the smartest, strongest or richest, so that game was not worth playing out. The key became manipulation, influencing, making people laugh, making deals, and bartering your way to success.

That's the good news. Now for the bad news. How can you be certain that your accounting department isn't hiding the truth inside the financials if you don't pay attention to the financials? How can you build standardization and system optimization if you value freedom over consistency? Ignoring these issues and a thousand other micro-details comes at the cost of developing a world-class culture.

Quadrant 3

Quadrant 3 is in the bottom left corner. People in Quadrant 3 are low on rules, systems, structures, policies and procedures. They are also low in communication, relationships, team-building and camaraderie. These people tend to solve problems through avoidance, addictions, and overreactions. Their greatest fear is being found out as lacking and losing their job or status. Their favorite activity is escapism. Quadrant 3 people are famous for making excuses, blaming others, and creating distractions. It's entirely possible for a Quadrant 3 person to have a legitimate mental health issue. Clearly, of the cars I mentioned at the beginning, the unmaintained, dirty truck full of old receipts is a Quadrant 3 car.

Most people, groups, companies and even countries have a hard time pulling out of Quadrant 3 on their own. The power of a team is often needed to even get the process started. Letting someone you know at work or home hit rock bottom is not an act of self-determinism but rather a lack of vision and skill for those who have the capacity to help.

The Quadrant 3 CEO didn't gain the corner office because the board valued Quadrant 3. He or she slid into Quadrant 3 due to a multitude of reasons, including burnout, mental health issues, fatigue, or moral erosion. Home stress may have contributed: a marriage break-up, family sickness or some other loss. Normal, natural healthy grief takes the best out of a Quadrant 2 CEO and can take you on a journey into the barren desert of Q3.

LOST IN THE FOG

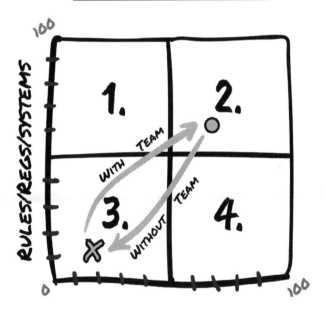

This is when it's time to reach out – and if you're the CEO, chances are you'll have to take that first step. Reach out to your private professionals: your family doctor, therapist, coach, mentor, whomever. Then reach out to your private family or friends you trust. If you have the right level of respect, trust, and a good relationship, you might reach out to the Chairman of the Board. Finally, reach out to your executive team.

What pushes a CEO into Quadrant 3 can be managed, shortened, and turned into incredible Quadrant 2 culture-building experiences for the company, you, and your family. Whatever you do, don't hide in your cave. Wandering through Quadrant 3 on your own is a high-stakes game.

Quadrant 2

At last we arrive to the promised land, Quadrant 2, at the top right of the diagram.

THE PROMISED LAND

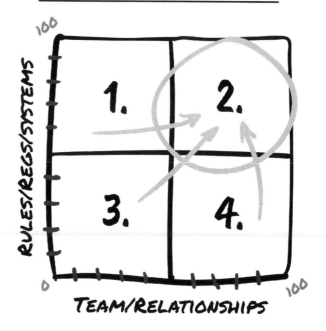

This is world-class. People in Quadrant 2 are high in rules, systems, structures, policies and procedures.

They are also high in communication, relationships, team-building and camaraderie. This is the new, four-door, six-cylinder truck in my parking lot. The family in this car cares about each other, and their possessions. They drive the right size car for the family, and the vehicle is well-maintained.

Most people, groups or companies do not naturally achieve Quadrant 2, and have to work hard to gain and maintain that Quadrant. Growing companies and advancing individuals often lose Quadrant 2 for a season every time their world changes due to growth and expansion. Why is this? It's because with growth you outgrow your existing rules, regulations, systems and, at the same time, your communication patterns and HR and team capacity. The strategy here is to anticipate the shift and plan ahead as best as possible. Limit the exposure of self and the company during the out-of-Quadrant 2-phase and shorten the time it takes you to climb back into the top right corner.

If you are a Quadrant 2 CEO, you're the total package. You have a high IQ as well as a high EQ (emotional intelligence) within a balanced and high performing team. Your job now is to stay humble, hungry and willing to mentor and inspire others to join you. If they do join you, your success will most likely push you out of Quadrant 2 and into a growth phase that you thought was reserved for the young and ambitious. Imagine yourself as this CEO, leading into your seventies or eighties with the knowledge that you are constantly having to innovate to keep yourself, your extended family, your company and your community leadership roles in a healthy and functional Quadrant 2. We would say you are living the dream.

The Real World

Now that you understand the basics of the 4 Quadrants, let's see how it all plays out in the real world. Recall that Quadrant 1 is all about the rules and regulations, all about the systems, but the people skills are not there at all. There is no warmth coming from a Quadrant 1 CEO, and they don't communicate effectively. As a result, there is no team; or, if there is team, its members don't like each other. Quadrant 3 is total breakdown, a deterioration of systems, a breakdown of relationships. This is where you're going to find a lot of pain and chaos.

As we have discovered, a lot of companies have actually set up their metrics to be in Quadrant 1. Most business data tracking focuses only on the Y axis. But they will never reach greatness, because they're missing a key ingredient: taking care of the culture.

For instance, it might look good on the books to centralize all of your offices and get out of regional areas, because you can optimize and won't have as much redundancy. However, when you pull your key personnel out of a community of 1,500 people or less, you've impacted that community significantly; their sports teams, policing, the hospital, the schools. You've got to look at the big picture. If you want your employees engaged and you want to be a benefit to society, you may find the answer is to not pull out of that small community. Quadrant 1 vs. Quadrant 2 thinking.

Another Quadrant 1 approach would be to contract everything out because you live in fear. The insurance companies will tell you every day to contract out everything where you're exposed to risk. If you're stirring chemical goo, get somebody else to do that. If you're jumping out of planes, get somebody else to do that. Don't do it yourself. Distance yourself from the liability. But is it the right thing to do? From a Quadrant 1 world view, it's fine. From a Quadrant 2 point of view you have to ask the deeper, wider questions: How does it impact the people? How does it impact the culture?

Quadrant 4 is what most people would call the "good old days." These were the days when workers didn't have to wear hard hats and kids didn't have to wear seat belts. As a result of no safety gear, a bunch of mine workers got long-term lung problems from airborne particulates. Some even died, but it was seen as part of the cost of coal mining. There was more freedom, in the sense of there being fewer regulations, but the result was not world class.

Then there's the case for the beer fridge in the lunch room. Who got rid of the beer fridge? The lawyers and the insurance companies. They said, sure, you can have your Quadrant 4 team by having a beer fridge in your operation. Do you have $5 million cash in the war chest? Because that's what it will cost if one of your employees smashes into the girls' volleyball team school bus on the way home after drinking alcohol on site.

So right now, there is a general trend of beer fridges getting taken out of lunch rooms around the globe. While I'm not advocating for the beer companies and actually don't even drink, getting rid of the beer fridge hurts most companies' morale. The Quadrant 1 CEO doesn't even consider the loss of team, because this CEO is just focused on risk management. The Quadrant 4 CEO grieves the loss but is not organized enough to build in new systems to replace the loss. The Quadrant 3 CEO just sits in his or her office and wonders why nothing seems to be going right.

To solve the beer fridge culture crisis you need to leverage both the X and Y axis of the 4 Quadrant diagram. You have to figure out how to achieve Q2 without the beer fridge. It's not about giving out turkeys and hats; it's deeper than that. You have to figure out how to engage the team in meaningful conversation and cooperation, collaboration –and not only the team, but your stakeholders, your investors, the board of directors...the whole gang.

You also have to leverage the rules and the systems to get all of these players to perform in a way that supports a Q2 culture. This may mean becoming less rules-centric and focusing on the achievement of both the x and y axes. The beer fridge is an example of a symptomatic trend in business. Most business have been pushed into Q1 and are in need of immediate change.

Creating Silos

It requires a hard right intervention to get from Quadrant 1 to Quadrant 2. If you are in Quadrant 1, your organization and your departments are going to be siloed, or isolated, because of a lack of relationships and team awareness. Important decisions aren't being shared, and there is a lack of trust. With that lack of trust come all kinds of breakdowns in efficiency. Engaging in a hard right turn into Q2 builds trust throughout the team, punches holes in silo walls, opens up communication and is really good for business.

The Corporate Silos Diagram illustrates how an organization's departments can end up outside of Quadrant 2 and as a result suffer and under-perform unnecessarily.

CORPORATE SILOS

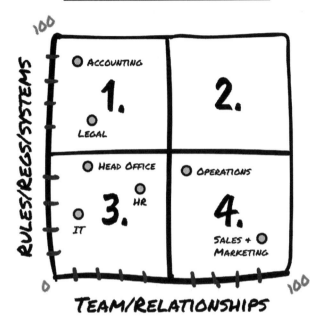

Implementing Switchback is a very effective way to build trust within teams, much more effective than going bowling with each other, or drinking to excess at the company picnic, or taking a high ropes team-building course. Don't waste your time and money on superficial distractions. Build real team in real time, in the real setting. We always insist that our Switchback training take place on site, even if it means three flights and a crew boat ride to a remote logging float camp. Now it's real. Imagine if we had run the same three-day training at a downtown hotel in a major city. The stories which build the culture, by the way, would have nothing to do with being real or Switchback training but rather involve the after-hours drinking shenanigans and other things people get up to when they're transplanted into a different setting.

The Quadrant system is one of the foundations of Switchback. We will refer back to it throughout the next development of Switchback thinking. This system is always in play, and as you read through the next chapters you'll see how the basics of the quadrants show up in many ways and interactions, regardless of the size of your company. The Quadrant system is a clear reminder that people are human, fluid in their choices and behaviors, and, more importantly, that people can change. Consider the 4 Quadrant system as a beacon, helping you set and measure targets on your journey of achievement and transformation.

Retirement Warning

Before advancing, however, let's stop for a moment and focus on retirement in light of the 4 Quadrant Diagram. Once you finally retire, all the stress, responsibility, and requirement to lead are somehow magically removed. Wait just a moment – what this would mean is that all the rules, systems, structures, policies and procedures, communication, relationships, team-building and camaraderie have all just been magically removed. The mistaken new target becomes Quadrant 4.

Sit down, relax, take it easy, catch your breath. As you settle into Q4, what is happening to your Quadrant trajectory? It most likely looks like a nice easy curved arrow from Quadrant 2 into Quadrant 4 and now headed to the bottom of Quadrant 3. If life is lived at its best in Quadrant 2 then life is lived at its worst in Quadrant 3.

RETIREMENT WISDOM

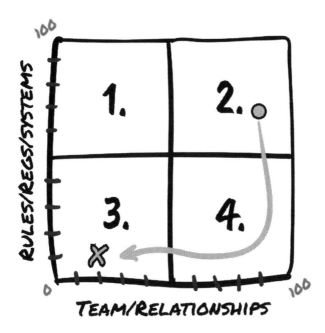

The solution, therefore, is to live life intentionally in every season: no free ride, ever. My aunt Margaret, at 91 years old, has more defined biceps, straighter posture and more friends than most people half her age, and we haven't even mentioned her laugh. She works out, lives in community and has a deep personal faith. Are you surprised she is still thriving at 91?

In retirement you need to build rules, systems, structures, policies and procedures, communication, relationships, team building and camaraderie. Try to go from being a successful CEO to a solitary basement fine woodworker and I will bet you'll be visiting Quadrant 3 in your not-so-distant future. You might be sick of systems and people, which is understandable, so your new journey is to find systems and people who don't make you sick and then join them, fully, with both feet in. You may not be the CEO but you will be back in structure and team and living life fully in Quadrant 2.

How to leverage the 4 Quadrant System:

As CEO your job is to keep your finger on the pulse of every moving part, trusting the experts and their reporting and giving overall direction in light of multiple factors. It's a complex job and we would like to make the human component easier for you. We have taken the 4 Quadrant System and made it into an easy-to-use pulse survey App. Through automation you can track your whole business, departments, specific teams and regions and learn how they are doing, how they think their teams are functioning and how the overall culture is doing. With this data we give you the opportunity to analyze, average, trend and report to your team the culture feedback of your employees. During intense change the pulse survey and reporting can happen every day. In less intense times in the life cycle of your organization you can pull back the question frequency. Our goal is to give you valuable data and reporting opportunities that will change how you and your team think about your organization's culture. You'll see that measuring culture can be a key driver for success.

Chapter 4

The Front and Back of the Brain

ONE THING I LEARNED OVER YEARS AS A FAMILY therapist is that people make a million excuses for bad behavior. They give a "good" reason for it, and then, just like a lawyer, they build a whole case that supports their beliefs, thoughts and actions. "Well, if you only knew my story, Steve," these clients often would begin, and away they'd go. As a family therapist, sixty-minute appointments with each of my rationalizing clients every week meant hours and hours of listening to excuses. Not my idea of a great profession.

That scenario is what led me to develop the skills I needed to help people cut through the whole excuse and justification cycle and identify early on what was the target they were shooting for. I'd ask them what was in their way, what documentation they had giving them the right to maintain their current position, and what would be the best-case scenario for a solution.

Then I asked them: How hard would it be to change that position to something that you would prefer? Together, we'd create an action plan, including action towards a change of belief so they could actually make some movement towards their preferred state of mind, their preferred state of relationship, or economic success, whatever the goal was.

Some would argue this approach is not empathetic, and fair point, because some people interpret empathy as the ability to sit in people's pain, chaos, and suffering... in other words, to let people go around and around on a hamster wheel in the back of their brain, talking in terms like "woe is me," and "this is why I'm allowed to be like this." Different strokes for different folks. I have always been more interested in helping people move forward, not spin their wheels.

I ran a very successful family therapy private practice by being less empathetic and more innovative and entrepreneurial, and this book reflects that. If you're looking for someone to just hold your hand and join the pain that you live in, you're going to have to find someone who is more of a hand-holder. If you're looking for a toolbox that challenges your current bad habits and shows you how to conquer these bad habits through neurological processing and understanding core beliefs, meta cognition, memory storage and systems thinking, you've found yourself a master expert in Switchback.

Here is my Switchback brain theory in summary.

Switchback Brain Theory

Understanding how the brain stores memories is the key to living in Quadrant 2 and being able to successfully aim high and execute our intentions.

It all starts with what I call "Xs." These Xs are the memories and limiting beliefs (which can be lies directed towards yourself or others) that are triggers and fire off when least expected, sending the brain into fight-or-flight mode just when you're presenting that memo to the board or driving the forklift of breakables up that ramp.

Brain experts say that all stimulus is stored in many parts of the brain. We know it's complex, so in Switchback, in order to make this a functional conversation, we focus on just two of the areas where memories are stored. One area we call the front of the brain to keep it simple, and the other area we call the back of the brain. Memory Xs are originally stored in the back of the brain because that's the only place where the brain can logically place them to keep them from interfering with what you have to do to survive. The back brain is the reactive, reptilian part of the brain, where the fight-or-flight stress response is activated. Memories that cannot be stored in the front of the brain due to their toxicity, trauma or startle factors are stored independently on the flight mountain at the back of your brain, in solitary vaults.

However, Xs can be moved from the back of the brain to the front of the brain. The front of the brain stores all the memories that are aligned with your success, resilience, and building of capacity. This bank of interacting front brain memories becomes the foundation of your life.

The Front of the Brain

This area holds your collective wisdom, also known as emotional intelligence (EQ). The more you operate and build up front brain dominance the better, because then you can look at a situation and read yourself, read the room, read the overall big picture, attune to what's happening, and navigate the situation more successfully. You can hold all of these memories in light of your history, your current circumstances, and what your hopes and dreams are for your company or for your family. From this place you then know what to do –or, if you realize you don't know, you know you need to expand your team to gain the expertise you need.

The front of the brain is set up to make you successful and as a result, stores memories aligned to that goal. While operating in the front brain, you can drift or be pushed out of the sweet spot for optimum success and end up in a continuum of passive thinking at one extreme and aggressive thinking at the other. Recognizing yourself and others on this continuum is a game changer.

Some people think it would be great if life were simple and all we had to deal with was front brain memory storage. But life isn't that simple. Even within our front rational brain, we can be pushed out of the sweet spot and process our life either through a passive or aggressive perspective. When a CEO operates outside of this front brain sweet spot the measurable result is a lack of true world class TEAM.

The Sweet Spot

In a perfect world, we would spend the majority of our time in neither passive nor aggressive thinking, but rather in that sweet spot we call "world class success," which is the circle in the middle below.

FRONT BRAIN MEMORY STORAGE

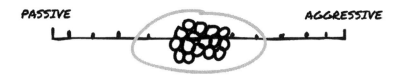

As I will illustrate later in this chapter, passive thinkers have been pushed out of that sweet spot due to circumstance and environmental pressure.

In the same way, aggressive thinkers have been pushed out of the sweet spot and are over-compensating with their aggressive thoughts and behaviors.

It is not uncommon for people's thoughts to be all over this continuum depending on their circumstances. One moment you may be in the sweet spot; the next moment you react into passive thinking; and the moment after that, you switch into aggressive thinking.

The Back of the Brain

I draw the back of the brain as two opposing mountains. The mountain on the left is the Flight Mountain. The mountain on the right is the Fight Mountain. I draw the Flight Mountain as a snow-capped mountain because the higher you climb it, the greater the risk of isolation, unhealthy and dysfunctional thinking and really a form of isolation and hypothermia.

At the peak of the other mountain, the Fight mountain, is an active volcano. If you get yourself worked up with back of the brain fight thinking, you could burn up yourself and others. It's a pretty bad neurological and social situation, really, on both mountains.

THE SWITCHBACK BRAIN

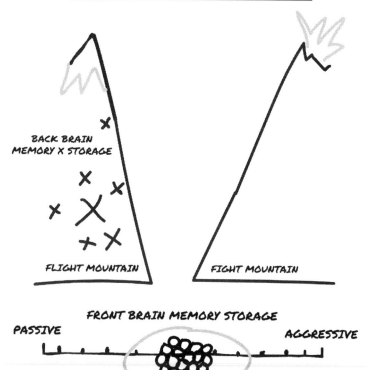

BACK BRAIN
MEMORY X STORAGE

FLIGHT MOUNTAIN

FIGHT MOUNTAIN

FRONT BRAIN MEMORY STORAGE

PASSIVE

AGGRESSIVE

Ideally, you want to process your life with your front brain; but some situations trigger memories that are stored in the back of your brain, creating a toss-up about whether you are going to respond with your front brain or react with your back brain. It happens in the board room, with your operations team, in traffic, and at home. You get a dump of adrenaline, or one of the other chemicals and hormones that make up the precise balancing act of your brain.

When everything is clicking along and running in your optimum preferred position, your chemicals and hormones balance your thought process in the front of your brain. When you're upset, however, they start pushing you out of the front of your brain. This is when you get the adrenaline dump. It drives your neurological processing to the back of your brain and now you're in flight-or-fight response.

POWER OF ADRENALINE

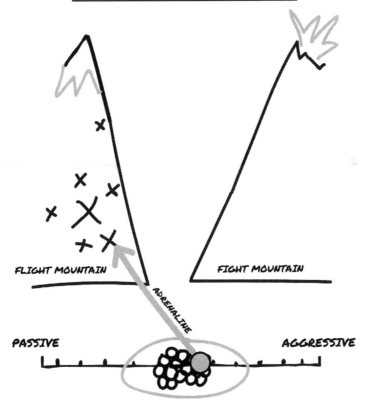

FLIGHT MOUNTAIN   FIGHT MOUNTAIN

ADRENALINE

PASSIVE   AGGRESSIVE

When it comes to the flight-or-fight response, after analyzing a couple of decades of client reactionary examples, I'm convinced that the first back of the brain reaction is flight. If something jumps out at you, the first thing you'll do is recoil. Then the next thing will be to either fight or freeze.

When we first began this work within industry, we came across two primary leadership pathways: the self-made leader who came up through the ranks, and the professional trained leaders who gained their status from a foundation in academia. Many of the self-made leaders identified their front brain default as aggressive and didn't understand either the flight side or the Memory Xs. They'd say things like, "I'm an aggressive leader, and when things don't go my way I switch to fight mode – to the death."

What about the leaders who went to university and were now in leadership positions shoulder to shoulder with the self-made leaders? Are they aggressive or passive by default? Interestingly, almost to a person, the university-trained leaders took a passive stance in their leadership style within the work culture. They could totally relate to the flight response. If you ask someone who tends towards the passive side on the front of their brain whether they can identify Xs, usually they'll answer in a way that reveals they are completely aware of their Xs. Not all of them, but they know that they exist. This is the world they live in.

Can you see how leadership tensions develop with these two contrasting leadership default settings? The self-made leaders act like bulls in the china shop without a lot of self or situational awareness, while the university-trained leaders back away from conflict, taking a passive stance in the front of their brains and spending a lot of brain power spinning self-doubt on the flight side of the back of the brain.

When these two groups of leaders gain a Switchback perspective to their challenging worlds, lights go on and transformation starts. The self-made leaders cool their jets, become more reflective and shift into creating a world-class team; and the university-trained leaders pick up their game, join the team and shift away from self-doubt. People can change.

UNDERSTANDING THE FLIGHT/FIGHT RESPONSE

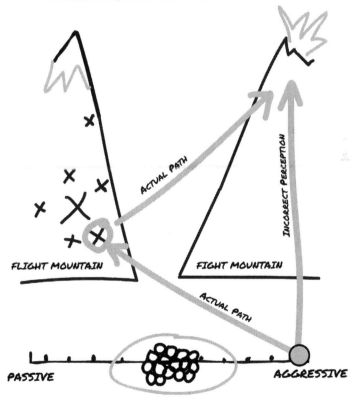

This is an example of what happens in our everyday human experience. Something triggers us at work, and the flight response is activated. If you are on the aggressive side, you'll fly across to Flight Mountain, pick up some memory Xs, and with lightning speed leave the flight response and head directly to your preferred fight response. Then you'll typically fail. You always hit an X first because that's the adrenaline-sponsored landing pad for the next neurological synapse that's going to happen in your brain.

The brain is always looking for landing pads for the synapse to touch on as it goes back and forth. This new landing pad may open up a memory X vault, or it may just land on a memory X and skip over to the fight response. Now your brain is firing on the fight response, but unfortunately, you're now fighting not with the front of the brain, which is rational, strong, and full of wisdom, but with your irrational side. You've got a little bit of a tear in your eye and your heart rate is elevated and you start to lose control. Consequently, you fail, which then drives you higher up the mountain.

The name Switchback is clearly demonstrated in the back of the brain. In an upsetting situation you switch from the flight to the fight, back to the flight and onward. This pattern is like a switchback trail ascending a steep mountain face.

The point is not to block this process from happening or to try to avoid it occurring. This happens to everybody all the time.

I love to watch professional ice hockey. You would be surprised how often even pro hockey players accidently crash into each other on the ice; it is part of the sport, playing hard on the edge and managing risk while 100% switched-on. Anyone who has run a business knows that the life of a CEO models a professional ice hockey game more than a fun round of golf with friends.

CLASSIC SWITCHBACKING

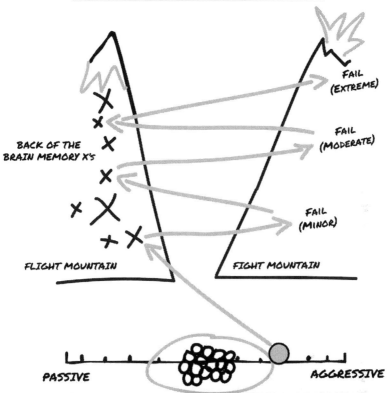

The point is to be able to anticipate the flight /fight reaction, recognize it early, minimize its effects, and create a culture where building mental capacity to manage stress is a top value. If people don't understand that success involves dealing with the back of the brain and the flight / fight response, they start self-pruning their lives.

Let's say, for example, that you go to Mexico on a holiday with your hard-earned money and there is a little scuffle in the evening on the way to your condo. You feel threatened, which causes you to lash out like you would back when you were a rowdy kid in high school. Here you are, a fifty-year-old man, and now you're acting like a punk and threatening somebody. Your brain knows that wasn't fun. It wasn't pleasure, it was pain. Then your brain decides what to do and makes a simple solution. Never go back to Mexico. Problem solved.

This is a terrible solution. A few months later, it happens again in Chicago. Next it happens at a Mariners game in Seattle. Before long, you start making your life smaller and smaller. This interplay happens consciously and unconsciously. We believe one of the keys to happiness and long-term success is managing our brain's desire to mitigate risk. But if you don't work every day to keep your life open and expanding you will naturally prune your life down, smaller and smaller until finally you're living in a condo and doing light bulb patrol at sixty-eight years old. Is that the life you want to live?

Choosing the quick fix, like just stopping trips to Mexico, doesn't get to the heart of what's causing the problem. The quick fix is usually chosen by people who are unwilling to engage in a bit of self-analysis. People who want to advance their careers will face their back-brain reactions again and again. Just wait until you get an off-shore partner and have to accommodate work habits founded in a different culture.

When you advance in your life, it is likely you will get pushed out of Quadrant 2. The systems aren't meeting the new needs and your communication and relationships are under stress. Lots of leaders at this moment pull back and stop growth because they sense that they have lost Quadrant 2. They're right: they have, but we know it can be just for a short season. If you can anticipate the temporary loss of Quadrant 2 and understand that old negative beliefs and thoughts like to re-establish themselves in moments like this, you can beat the negative pull-back that occurs with change.

This whole process of leaving team and becoming passive or aggressive or leaving team and switchbacking up the flight and fight mountains is not driven by personality. The driver is how your brain responds to stimulus. When you understand that your life does not have to be boxed in through personality profiling, you can then start setting your intentions towards a life that you want to live and a leadership style that really builds team.

Memory Xs Left Alone

What happens when people don't process and deal with their memory Xs, letting them fester and build thought processes that are dysfunctional, unhealthy and dangerous? On the flight side, the dominant activity is self-rejecting thinking, and on the fight side the dominant activity is rebellious thinking. The extremes of these are suicide and murder.

I've had real-life experience with this extreme switchback activity. We had an incident with one of our corporate clients right in the middle of a three-day training. All of a sudden, at around 10:15 am, people were going to their phones and looking agitated. Rather than thinking we could just power through the distraction, we asked the obvious question, "Is something not right? Should we pause and focus on what's coming through your phones?"

We stopped the training and shifted focus. There was a developing incident; an active shooter at one of their sites. When the dust cleared we could plot the incident on the Brain Diagram. An unhappy worker outside of team on the passive side worked up the Flight Mountain, picking up Memory Xs along the way while losing rational control of his thinking. Without anyone knowing the risk, he switched from the top of Flight Mountain to the top of Fight Mountain and became an active shooter. There were fatalities.

ACTIVE SHOOTER

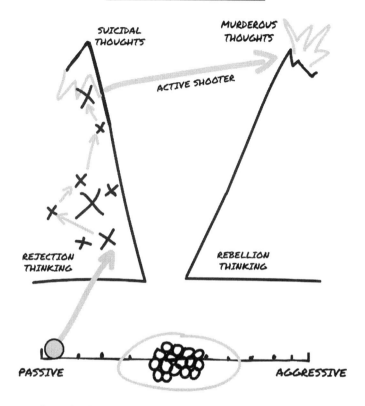

The Flight Mountain is the home for self-rejection thinking. As you climb up the mountain, it becomes more unhealthy, isolated, and irrational, leading ultimately to suicidal thinking. The Fight Mountain is home to rebellious thinking. These thoughts also escalate as you climb this mountain from simple negativity and blaming to conspiracy thinking all the way to murderous thinking.

Old memory Xs that have not been processed and moved can become active, and memory Xs that you have managed to move to the front of the brain can try to re-establish their territory back on the Flight Mountain. Attached to every memory X is a limiting belief. For example, one bad deal with a foreign bank 10 years ago created a memory X which in turn can build a limiting belief that sounds like, "Never trust foreign money: it will always burn you." Or even broader, "Never trust foreigners."

You can get some pretty strong limiting beliefs coming into your brain saying you shouldn't be doing this, you've overstepped, this isn't going to work out, this could be a career killing move, and all the rest. You don't have to listen to those voices; just ask yourself where those thoughts are coming from.

LIMITING BELIEFS

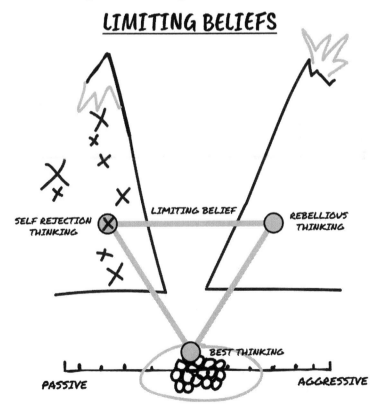

Metacognition

Switchback offers a way for people to switch their brains on and learn to manage their thinking. It's called meta-cognition and it involves thinking about your thoughts and analyzing them. Every thought is not to be taken at face value. Some of your thinking is brilliant. Some of your thinking is completely irrational. Learn how to discern the difference between what's brilliant and what's crazy. If you can do that, you can minimize the collateral damage of crazy thinking, and you can advance your life.

Here is an example, not only of how we apply Switchback, but also of how these Xs evolve over the years.

Imagine: There you are, a CEO, and you're off on a great little ski weekend with your family, including your three kids in their car seats in the back of your SUV. Everything should be perfect about this moment because you've got money, time, health and a family. How much better does it get? (I would suggest adding God for the ultimate ride but that's for a whole other book).

Suddenly, as you drive around a corner you notice a flare in the road. Instantly you know that something's up. After the flare, you see the blinking lights and your sensory perception gets switched-on. You see the ambulance door open, the stretcher, and the black body bag and you notice there are no barriers blocking the view. What are you going to tell the kids in the back seat to do?

Quite likely, you'll encourage your kids in a kind but firm tone (Quadrant 2, firm and friendly), to close their eyes. Just about every loving parent in the world would say that to their kids, because they don't want them to be scared or traumatized. We know that the brains of our children are not going to be able to absorb that stimulus and store the accident scene in a place that's useful. It's going to be stored in a place that could trigger them in the future – and who knows how and when. The medical community calls these brain/behavioral conditions Adverse Childhood Experiences (ACE).

As the parent, you've asked your kids to close their eyes. Your two daughters, who also happen to be great students, do as you've asked. Your son, however, who is uncoordinated, distracted, and quite possibly waiting for an attention-deficit disorder diagnosis, is going to do what? You guessed it, he's going to look. He's going to look because doing so gives him a shot of adrenaline and he has conditioned his brain to hunger for the adrenaline and feed off the upset condition.

He needs that shot because it puts him into his place of familiarity, which is the back of the brain, switching between the flight and fight response. That's where he learned to distract himself, some would say cope, because he's not meeting expectations. He's not fitting into the team, which is something he's picked up from his parents, teachers, and coaches. But he has a place he can go to get the stimulation he seeks.

He looks out the window and between what's real and what he perceives, he thinks he sees an arm on the road. This lights his brain up even more, it's his cocaine for the moment. Now, how will this kid be coping on Monday during his math test? Distracted. How will his ability to socializing during lunch hour be? Not good. His sleep patterns? Not great. All of these things are affected by his need to stay in his back-brain place of stimulation.

Let's roll this forward 20 years. Now your son has stumbled through university and he's trying to find his way. He's employed by a company similar to yours and

77

he's trying to do a good job. He's trying to operate out of the front of his brain, but he's got a lot of memory Xs stored in the back of his brain, memories of those car accidents and the barking dogs and teachers and coaches telling him if he'd only focus, he'd amount to something. With these memories come thoughts of disappointment and shame, among others.

At this moment as a 30-year-old, he is a gifted and talented underachiever. However, he is still part of a company, so he is both an asset (gifted) and a liability (underachiever). This goes for every single person working in your company. Part of their brain is an asset, and part of their brain is a liability.

The connection between stimulus, memory Xs and response is not always a solid line. In fact, it is often not even a dotted line, because it involves the brain and the brain is complex. However, while this son, all grown up, is driving the company vehicle something triggers him and switches him into the back of his brain, opening the vault from the memory of that day in the back of your SUV. All of a sudden, a percentage of his brain is hamster wheeling and ruminating on that moment when he thought he saw the arm on the road.

Meanwhile, he's also driving, and he's got three crew members in that same vehicle heading to the job site. This is when Switchback really becomes boots-on-the-ground practical for your workforce. If he has the understanding of a working model like Switchback as a way of reading his internal signs, listening to his thoughts and interpreting what's going on, then he can apply metacognition and control the outcome of his next actions.

If he were skilled in Switchback, he might turn to his colleagues in the truck and tell them he just hit an X.

The guys in the truck might ask him what the X was, and he'd tell them about the SUV, the accident, how his dad told him not to look and how he thought he saw an arm on the road. By doing that, he's externalizing the memory, and his front brain is taking charge of the moment and controlling the outcomes. The guys in the truck might ask him where the X is living now, and he'd think it through and tell them it's still living in the back of his brain because he literally had not thought about this memory for years and to his knowledge had never front-brain processed the memory.

If his co-workers had taken a Switchback training, they'd ask him if he was okay and offer to drive. Just acknowledging that as an option is often enough. He might take them up on it, or not, or just want to talk it through. They would encourage the dialogue.

They'd listen to him figure it all out; making the connections between what was happening in his life at the time, how his parents were disappointed in him, how his sisters were "perfect." How he was confused and unsure of his identity. All of this could be talked through, step by step in logical order, as he drives his colleagues to a job site, on an otherwise normal day.

As he continues to process, he would recognize that the X is actually clustered beside a number of other Xs that happened at the same time; the story goes on. The whole conversation from triggering the X to wrapping it up could have taken less than three minutes, which is safe, efficient and amazing.

Switchback training teaches staff to work together in situations like the one I just described, where the moment a teammate is triggered, the team can communicate and help move the X with that person. The team communicates, and the office becomes a practical place to talk about these Xs. A company that has taken Switchback training will now have the skills to not only handle moving Xs in acute, triggered moments, but also how to get ahead of Xs. We do this by instilling a culture of weekly check-ins. For companies that have embedded Switchback training and thinking into their culture, these check-ins are a normal, brief conversation on any given day.

Using the Switchback method and check-ins leaves you with a switched-on workforce that's doing some pretty significant peer support in each other's lives and then rolling it forward, so that same conversation happens when people go through divorces or lose their parents, and all the rest. You'll have a company where people are actually looking forward to Monday morning and looking forward to that three-minute chat or that drive to the work site, or that chance to huddle together in accounting where they do their check-ins.

In this system, a typical Switchback check-in might include blending in a little small talk with operational topics and what's impacting people lives right now. With a couple of questions, you can help people understand if this will affect their work, or if they need to make any shifts that day. Usually the person will not need accommodation because just being supported by their team is enough.

You can't buy engagement, you really can't. You can give a professional athlete a ten- million-dollar contract and they can choose not to engage. If you can give an athlete a ten-million-dollar contract without a guarantee of engagement, then an eighty-thousand-dollar salary isn't going to motivate people to engage. What engages them is when you offer a culture that is organized, structured, and warm, along with tools to help them understand their thoughts and a culture of care and support within all departments, from accounting to legal to HR to operations.

Imagine sitting in your office with the door open and hearing your Monday morning Switchback check-ins taking place, reverberating throughout the building. That is the dream for just about any CEO I can think of, because you've got yourself a switched-on organization. They are switched-on because you are a switched-on CEO and people are inspired by and mirror their leader's thoughts and actions.

Chapter 5

Finding and Moving Memory Xs

NOW THAT YOU HAVE AN UNDERSTANDING OF WHAT runs in the background of your brain and the brains of your employees, what do we do with this? Beyond just cultivating a deeper sense of knowing ourselves and greater empathy for the struggles of our team, we can actually apply this understanding to finding and moving Xs in the moment. This is the real juice, the change agent.

With our Switchback theory, based on neuroscience, you can harvest any X in the back of your brain and move it to the front of your brain. Some Xs are very hard to process and will continue to have a consequence in your life and will never turn to lemonade and will forever be a lemon. Even so, it is far better to have control and understanding over the Xs within the safety of the front of the brain, than to leave them in the back of the brain where they can sabotage your life. Some Xs can be moved to the front of your brain, transformed and become a real asset to your life. There are some Xs that have silver linings and some that do not. But, the truth is that you can move any memory from the back brain to the front brain and have it managed and kept safe by your incredible package of front brain emotional and intellectual maturity and capacity.

We want to move the Memory Xs from the back of the brain to the front in order to gain front brain control over the Memory X. We want to change the isolated status the X has by using our front brain wisdom, empathy, and understanding. We are ultimately building resilience by managing, uncovering, acknowledging, moving, and deeply understanding Memory Xs with the front brain and with the help of team.

Managing our Memory Xs this way also provides the added benefit of improved health and wellness, since it limits our exposure to the toxic release of chemicals and hormones that happens through contact with the back of the brain. We also have an increased capacity to grow and develop, as Xs hidden in caves and vaults in the back of the brain can really put the brakes on personal growth and career development. Possibly the biggest benefit to finding and moving our Xs is the transformation process of ending limiting beliefs and gaining new beliefs that are based on front brain truth and wisdom. This process can change your self-identity and create a positive effect in your mind and body that ripples out into your inter-actions with others.

Finding memory Xs is like a treasure hunt. Step one is aligning your brain in the right place to do the work. The best word for that is perceiving the work as "fasci-nating." If you approach moving Xs from a place of hope-lessness or difficulty, or stressful, anxiety-driven duty, you're actually triggering and activating the back of your brain, where the limiting beliefs live.

Imagine a holiday Memory X treasure hunt. There you are, a CEO, at your mother's place in Florida for Christ-mas and you not only just acted like a 14-year-old, you recognized it. Fascinating. You're sitting on the squeaky bed in your bedroom, stripped of all your power and authority and awesomeness you ordinarily have at work, and you're asking yourself the question, "What just hap-pened?" Set your brain on "fascinating." Be fascinated rather than frustrated. What was the current stimulus that triggered it? Start there. It was when your mom said, "Come on, don't be silly." Specifically, it was the word "silly."

"You're embarrassing us," she said. "Don't be silly." Consider, why did the word "silly" trigger you? Wait for it, and in time, your brain will give you the X, some-times in the moment, sometimes after processing with a number of people. And then you recall the memory. She called you silly in front of your friends. It happened in the living room. You were sitting on your dad's Lazy-boy. At the time you laughed it off, but also wondered if your friends were able to see your shame. You'll think it's crazy, because you won't have thought of it in years, but that's the X.

HISTORICAL MEMORY X'S

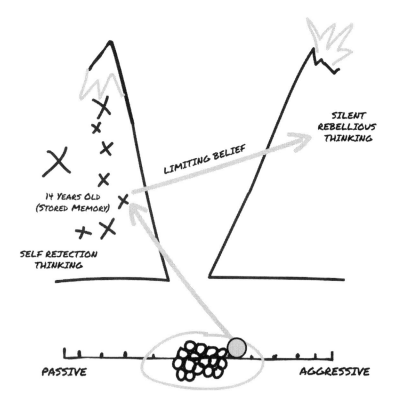

Is it a current threat? The answer is no. Is it a perceived or real threat? Well, that's different. At the time it was very real, but now it is a perceived threat. Your mother is in her early 80s and you are in your 50s, so why are you still reacting like a 14-year-old? Only because you haven't moved the X.

Is that X movable? Absolutely. But there's one more piece that would be really fascinating to sort out, which would be what is the limiting belief attached to that X? Just ponder that for a minute. Ask why. What is the limiting belief? It's like a triangle: your desired response is from the front brain, the X is what sabotaged it, the limiting belief is what supports the sabotage.

In this case, the limiting belief might be that you do not trust authority figures completely because you never know when they might call you silly in front of your peers. This limiting belief is reinforced by your mom never acknowledging your success, which hurts you because you've been wanting to hear your mother tell you she sees you as successful your whole life. When she says, "don't be silly," she's not acknowledging your achievements. She is not acknowledging the transformation that has occurred in your life, and this makes your blood boil.

Now you've gone from thinking, *you've got to be kidding me, that is a deeply hurtful thing to say, even though it sounds so innocent,* to, *something's going to die. If I could just pop your head off right now, I would.* This is what your inner thinking process says. Instead, you give your mother a look that says *I wish you were dead*—just for a micro-second. (Note: This is why paying attention to the micro-expressions with your executive team and board is mission-critical. Develop the skill to see them, and become fascinated with the process.)

Later, you can't believe you acted like a rebellious teenager. You're a 54-year-old CEO running a half-billion-dollar company and you gave your mom the dead eye? But now you've got it. Now you've captured this thing. Now you can just move it down. How? By talking about it. You find the five people who are your trusted top peer supporters. Your spouse, one of your adult kids. Maybe it's one of your colleagues at work.

Maybe it's your brother, because your brother may have had a similar experience to you. And you just talk about it.

This is a very practical step-by-step process which you can document so you can measure your success. Wouldn't it be fantastic to be able to love your elderly mother, regardless of her choice of words and her lack of acknowledgment, without the liability of Xs sabotaging you and your relationships?

It is common for motivational gurus to teach people to drop their negative friends and family and only hang out with positive people, like themselves. This is actually poor advice. I suggest an alternative. Become mentally tough, sort out your memory Xs, challenge your limiting beliefs, and then be a shining example to your friends and family regardless of whether they are negative. To be world class we have to sort out our past and not run from it.

Keep Searching

That's one way of finding your X. Another way is to take note when you have a reaction you're not proud of; this means that you switched to the back of your brain. Maybe you procrastinated or you didn't meet a deadline. You don't recognize yourself: it's so out of character to do that. You start looking for an X.

Perhaps you're sitting in your CEO office looking at the big picture of your life and seeing where you missed some of your primary expectations. Maybe you're wondering how you gained 100 pounds all of a sudden. You're a rock star at work, yet with your personal health you're out of control. You might start looking for an X. You don't have to find the X right away, however. What you can do is find the system that's going to start helping you build momentum, which is a front-of-the-brain system development.

You can activate that shift by calling on your team. No one loses weight on their own. There are so many awesome teams available that you can join. Some cost money and some don't. Some are personal trainers and personal nutritionists, and some aren't. Don't worry about finding your X. Rather, set your achievement targets, set your transformational targets and make them a priority. While you are achieving and transforming your thinking and habits I guarantee your back brain memory Xs will come to light. And with the power of your front brain momentum you can process and move these Xs.

Another way is to search through your core beliefs to find the limiting belief that's holding you back – even if you don't know what the trigger Xs are. The X might actually be hidden on purpose because your brain is trying to manage all the balls you have in the air right now.

Your brain says, "This is not the time or the place or the season to uncover this X, however you are welcome to work on the limiting belief." The limiting belief is something that's become a core value, such as, "I am not lovable," or, "I don't measure up," or, "My body is not my greatest asset."" You find that limiting belief and then ask yourself the simple question, "What is the truth?" The truth is more powerful than the limiting belief.

HIDDEN MEMORY X'S

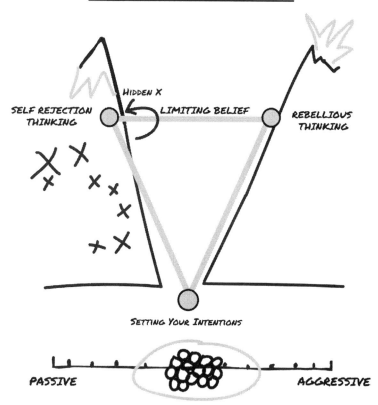

Moving the X

Finding Xs is all well and good, but now you're probably wondering how you actually move these Xs. We now have a clear understanding that memories are stored in different parts of the brain, that the back of the brain essentially stores trauma memories that we call Xs, and that those Xs become the trigger points, or the landing pads, for the flight/ fight reactions. So, how do you move an X?

MOVING MEMORY X'S

One way is through a process of externalization, like hovering in a helicopter over your life. I've interviewed professional athletes who have trained their brains to slow things down and almost get a secondary view of the situation, like being in a helicopter hovering 30 feet up from the action and looking down at what's going on.

My son, who played high level minor hockey, told me that in the heat of the moment things actually slow down rather than speed up for him. This is really just being switched-on. For my son, whenever he played hockey, he was entirely switched-on. It was as if he was able to hover over the upset condition in the heat of the moment and make front brain decisions while the rest of us were in the flight /fight reaction.

Just think about the advantage you would have with your team at work and your mother in Florida if you developed the ability to hover in the heat of the moment above your circumstances and take in other people's perspectives, or just have a wider view of the situation. Capturing and managing Xs becomes a lot easier when you can slow things down.

In the same way, you need to be able to capture your Xs, because right now they are essentially hiding from your rational brain. The best way to move Xs is to speak them out and write them out. We have found over the years that people who do this in private have less success than people who involve others in the process. You can hire professionals to help you harvest Xs, or you can build out peer support to help you.

We suggest you look at the entire network around you and pick five people who you think have the integrity and ability to talk about your Xs. It could be relatives, friends, or colleagues, and each person will have varying capacity to handle different parts of your life. In my own life, at one point my brother and I felt trapped in our careers. I was a family therapist and he was a minister, and neither of us had a trusted network to talk to. We were both in roles of authority, and roles in which it is inappropriate to unload your Xs on your clients. We also didn't want to unload with just anybody. We decided to book time once a month to go for a nice, long strategic walk. We both had a lot of junk from our childhood that needed to be sorted out. A lot of this was my torment of him, so we would start our walk and eventually one of us would shift the conversation and say, "So, you got anything?" And, the other would say, "No." "Yeah, me neither." We'd walk a little further, however, and inevitably something would come up.

When you are about to unload Xs, you often come up against your brain asking if this is the opportunity; if it's safe or if the environment is trustworthy. If it is safe and trustworthy, your brain will release a memory to you. Your brain is not going to give you 1,500 memory Xs at once because survival is the most important thing. It's going to tuck those things away privately where you will never remember them as long as you are in a state of orange alert.

If you are in orange alert your whole life, you will never process your Xs because your brain will protect you from them. If you are relatively front brain happy in your life, but you are still being sabotaged by the switch-back experience of going to the back of your brain, then it's time to find a walking partner, or peer support.

Once, when we were on our walk, my brother exclaimed, "Steve, I haven't thought about this for years!" Wasn't that an indicator that he had found himself an X that day?

The memory tumbled out quickly after that. In this instance, the memory was of a time when he was a teen and snuck under the fence at the local stock car races. My brother wasn't into lying or sneaking around, but he had an influential friend, and in the heat of the moment, mixed with his own teenage insecurities and trying to fit in, his back brain thinking tricked him into compromising his own morals and ethics. He and his friend slid under the fence and watched the races. My brother felt sick to his stomach that day; his front brain couldn't process what he had done, even though it was really quite innocent in the big picture. He tucked it away in his back brain as an X, and that day on our walk was the first time he'd thought about it in years.

I asked what he was going to do with this X, and he said he was going to pay the money back to the race track. We knew the owner, and when he approached him and came clean, the owner didn't want to take his money. Eventually, he took the money, and my brother drove home clear-minded with the X now moved to the front of his brain. The physical exchange of money, the externalization of the X and the walk all contributed to the successful moving of the X.

That's one way of moving Xs. We also recommend that people log the process. If you read peoples diaries, a lot of content is complaining and blaming. This log book is radically different. I would record the Xs, limiting beliefs and front brain intentions; and then the step by step process of moving the Xs, canceling the limiting beliefs, and realizing the intentions. It might take 50 conversations like my brother and I had regarding the race track before the X actually works its way permanently to the front of the brain. Is that too steep a price to pay? A conversation with your spouse, talking to a good friend, seeking out an expert online, reading a book on the topic, sorting out a few things, logging it on your cell, hiring someone to help you for just a couple of sessions to talk it through; is it worth it?

The truth is, once you've talked it through 50 times, it's likely that X will have lost its independent power in the back of your brain and will have found a new home in the front of your brain. I'm not saying that it's all going to be rainbows and unicorns, because some Xs are just plain old bad, and evil does exist on this planet. If you've been confronted with evil, it still has a consequence in your life. Where do you want to store the memory? You want to store it in the front where you can manage it.

The example I shared of my brother and me shows how it works to move an X in your personal life with the help of a trusted ally. I've witnessed hundreds of people move Xs right on the spot, during training events. This is profoundly effective, not only for the person, obviously, but for the group that witnesses moving an X in real time.

We held a Switchback training with an elite police force: all men, strong, confidant and on guard. One man was particularly on guard. He sat in uniform the entire time – and without touching the back of his chair for three days. He was on red alert.

As we went through the diagrams, teaching about moving Xs, we shifted the room from a training to a communications lab. A lab meant they had the opportunity to participate. And participating meant coming up with examples of Xs, where they were stored, and their interference with their professionalism.

This particular participant, through our process of building trust, finally decided to go for it and fully engage. He talked about a powerful incident that had produced a big impact in him; one wherein his boss basically threw him and the rest of his team under the bus. This wasn't anything close to as dramatic as things can get in his line of work; it wasn't a war zone setting, it wasn't shooting a bad guy. Shooting bad guys is his job! All of the men were trained to protect people and ready to lay down their lives for the team, for a friend. But they were not prepared to be betrayed by leadership.

Betrayal was at the root of his X, and it was powerful. He left the team after the betrayal, but who paid the price? Not only his colleagues but himself and his family. His brain did not know how to process the X, so it locked it up in a vault in the back of his brain.

You can move Xs, and it works. This particular man went in front of the room and told his story. I saw, halfway through, the micro-expression. Just as a side note – this is why you pay attention at meetings. Something in this man's demeanor went dark, for a nanosecond, and I saw it flash through his face, then he glanced at the exit.

He started to make a move. Remember, these were trained elite law enforcement professionals. They have specialized training. We were prepared with our own specialized training and understanding of the human factor. We are trained to build team and watch team. We are observers. I was on a rolling chair, and I made a tactical move. I rolled into the line of fire. I knew that if he walked out that door, he was potentially walking out of his career, his family, and potentially his life.

Sometimes you have to be willing to roll your chair into the line of fire. I rolled my chair in front of him, blocking the door surreptitiously, and with the kindest, firmest Quadrant 2 eyes that I could produce, I asked him to just hold on. Just a minute. I could tell he was at that crossroads. Life or death. We hold it in our hands, life and death. People are choosing, making the choices every day, life or death. I knew if I didn't roll in the way and represent life for him, that he was going to walk down a dark path. Life and death are in the hands of leaders. It's the stress of too much, right? It's the back of the brain, it's irrational. If you ratchet it up with a come-along to the top of the mountain, it actually seems like the right answer.

I rolled my chair in front of him and one of his buddies got up and encouraged him to continue. He stopped, took a couple of combat breaths– – deep, slow controlled breaths – calmed down and got himself back in. He might have had no more than 15% control of the situation with the front of his brain, but with the help of team he was able to finish his story and regain 80% control of his thinking.

Together, we watched the X move. His buddies were totally inspired. If he could talk about his X, they realized so could they. A whole new world of life was opening up for the room. This is something we witness every time we do Switchback. Within their own contexts, people are making game-changing moves.

This kind of powerful transformation is possible for you and your team, too. You just need to apply the Switchback System.

PART 2

Applying the Switchback System

Chapter 6

Setting Targets

As referenced in the introduction, the Switchback battle cry is:

People can change
The power of success is in team

In order to become a Switched-On CEO, you first and foremost need to believe that people can change. Yes, you can change!

Part of what we're doing with Switchback involves working with the concept of neuroplasticity. However, our style in Switchback, which is kind of our country charm and has helped us become a global company, is that we don't get into the medical or the psychological or the brain science debate. At the end of the day it is the transformational implementation that we measure rather than the size of anyone's vocabulary.

Part of working with this belief in neuroplasticity – the idea that people can change – involves setting your targets, aiming high, and doing this all with clear intention.

Setting targets focuses you on your path and aiming higher is a way of ensuring excellence. Setting intentions takes the entire experience to a deeper level. Sure, you could say "But Steve, isn't this just Goal-Setting 101?" and on some level, we are talking about goals. With Switchback, however, we want to deepen the goal-setting experience; we want to help you gain new clarity with high targets that have a foundation of strong and meaningful intention beneath them. We are elevating the classic SMART (specific, measurable, actionable, relevant, and timely) process to a whole new level by setting targets this way and doing it in concert with the Quadrant system, outlined in chapter three and drawn below.

THE FOUR QUADRANTS

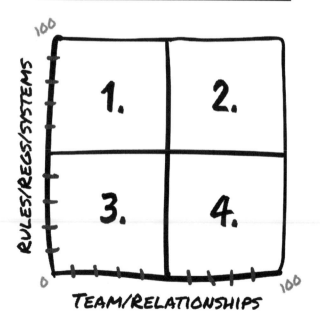

The practical way to set targets and aim high using the Quadrant system is to do a system analysis and ask which part of the system is in Quadrant 2, and which part of the system is out of Quadrant 2. To help people do this in family therapy, I encouraged them to draw a life map, which is basically a map with themselves at the center and everything that makes up their lives in the circle around them: family, work, hobby, exercise, faith, etc.

In a corporate setting, you may draw a corporate version of the life map and have all of your departments and operations as the aspects in this case. For either life map, you then look at every aspect and assess which quadrant you are in with regard to those aspects. You may observe that your executive team is in Quadrant 1, IT is in Quadrant 3, accounting is in low Quadrant 2 and your human resources department is in Quadrant 4. When you do this kind of analysis, you can then set targets for change.

While the positive thinking movement has tremendous value for people, I think the Switchback integrated model, where you're actually addressing and processing your pain and chaos as well as building positive capacity, is the true sustainable Quadrant 2 success model. For that reason, we need to be continuously setting targets. You can set professional targets, personal targets, team targets, and corporate targets, and then break each one down into specific areas. What you measure is where you give value. Our Switchback app is the perfect tool for organizations to measure, record and analyze this very important cultural component.

One of my favorite CEOs is from Australasia. He set the following clear, transformational, and intentional target for companies that he leads: "We will be the reasonable person in the room." When a company sets a standard of conduct, people end up rising to the challenge and taking their game to the next level. In any size company, whether it's 100 or 20,000 employees, there are a variety of ways that people interpret what 'appropriate' is. One of the core benefits of setting clear targets and intentions for both achievement and transformational goals is that people clearly know what the target is.

Without that target, you have cultural misalignment. You think you have the target set in bedrock, coming from corporate headquarters, but by the time that same value statement is interpreted out in the field, you can't even recognize it. It's like the old game of Broken Telephone kids used to play at parties, where the first kid whispers "monkeys like to eat bananas" in the next kid's ear, and by the time it gets back around the circle to her, she hears "funky bikes tweeted Nana." It breaks down somewhere in the transmission.

This is what's happening to your value statements and some of the targets that are coming out of head office right now, like "monkeys like to eat bananas," sound completely different by the time they get to the night shift at the sawmill. It's not just enough to have targets; you have to find a way to communicate company expectations in a way that the targets or expectations don't get inappropriately modified to suit people's own preferences. That's what strong Q2 leadership looks like.

Be sure that the target you're setting is actually where you want the entire company to go. It pays to do some heavy thinking around where the target is. Is it really in Quadrant 2 as opposed to Quadrant 1? There was a time when people thought Quadrant 4 was completely acceptable for company culture. There was a time when people thought it was completely acceptable for leaders to step outside of team and be very aggressive. There was also a time when not caring for each other was totally acceptable and a caring company culture was seen as overreach.

Employees shrugged it off and said they were just there for a paycheck and it was no one else's business what went on in their personal lives.

It's now common sense: people's personal lives completely affect their performance at work, so it is our responsibility to build a work culture that looks after people. Having something like Switchback gives you the opportunity to embed cultural principles deep down through your company, hold people accountable to the same message and not have this commitment fall victim to cultural drift or misalignment.

Clear targets are absolutely vital. The reason people often don't want to set clear targets is that they have deficiencies in their own lives. They say, "Who am I to hold somebody accountable to something that I can't achieve myself?" The truth is, a leader who is willing to talk about the journey and not just celebrate the destination is a high-quality leader. I admit that I default into all of the three quadrants quite easily when I'm off my game, so who am I to set a target of Quadrant 2 for the people who are part of my world? But who am I not to? Just because I'm not able to maintain Quadrant 2 all of the time doesn't mean it's not a valuable target.

Humans are complex. At any moment, something can happen that momentarily sabotages our better judgment. This is the reality of humanity. This does not excuse us from setting world-class targets. Targets have the ability to supersede human folly and we can be completely honest about the gap between our nature and our goals. We can acknowledge what our personal targets are and that we don't reach them daily or weekly, yet we maintain them as targets because we know doing so will bring us closer to the results we seek.

The Two Types of Targets

At Switchback, we break targets into two categories: achievement targets (the Y axis) and transformational targets (the X axis). Achievement targets are really awesome. They're basically typical goals: I want to lose 20 pounds, I want to save more money, I want to go on longer holidays. I want to eat healthier. These are targets that are achievement-oriented.

As a CEO, you have achievement targets embedded in your day-to-day operational language and actions. Monday morning production calls are all about action and achievement. Those reporting to you and your reports to the board are predominantly linear, step-by-step achievement reporting. Most bonuses and employee performance evaluations are based on achievement targets.

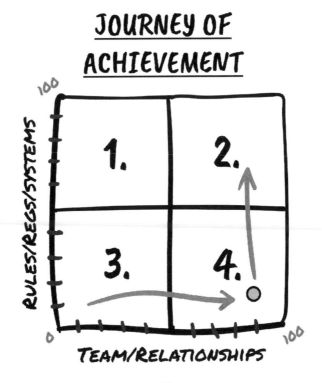

JOURNEY OF ACHIEVEMENT

An example of the journey of achievement is the digital advancement of recording and reporting in the corporate world. Imagine a CEO today who has not kept up to date with technology; who has no cellphone, can't type, can't open emails, can't build a PowerPoint presentation. You can find examples of highly successful business leaders who seem to maintain relevance without the journey of continuous digital achievement, but they are an anomaly and not the standard to strive for. At work, at home and in the community, we are constantly being challenged to maintain a steady pace of achievement.

The journey of achievement ideally propels you towards Quadrant 2, as you can see on the diagram. Even if a seasoned professional is brought on as a new CEO, if she's new to the industry itself she enters the role in Quadrant 3. If she is wise, she will listen and learn in order to gain the team's wisdom and insights so she can learn how to lead from Quadrant 2.

Integration into a new senior role is more difficult if the person comes in with high personal confidence, operational directedness and/or low industry knowledge. Many CEOs achieved early success in their careers by their technical skills and abilities as demonstrated on the Y axis of the 4-Quadrant diagram. The journey to Quadrant 2 in this case will be made smoother and faster by the CEO's willingness to also become an expert in the area of relationships and team. A company we work with just launched a new organizational structure combining 12 business units into 4 regions. The C suite is working overtime on the X axis keeping their employees understanding the changes, communicating the benefits and maintaining team and relationships.

Transformational targets are more difficult to understand. These are on the X-axis of the four quadrants, and are harder to measure compared to achievement targets. These are targets oriented to culture: values, trust, resilience, mental toughness under pressure, and work-life balance.

JOURNEY OF TRANSFORMATION

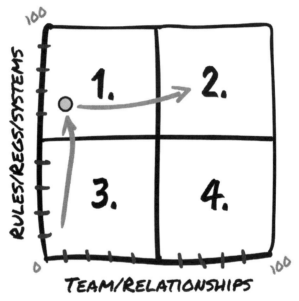

The CEO who finds herself in the corner office through the hard work of achievement without the equally important development of a personal and professional journey of transformation will quickly find that her tool box to lead is half empty.

The diagram "Journey of Transformation" illustrates this point. As she rose through the organizational chart, the new CEO achieved operational results (from Quadrant 3-1) which opened up the opportunity to advance. Leadership also requires the difficult and self reflective journey of transformation, however. The journey of transformation here requires stepping back; gaining wisdom; stop pushing; pausing; reflecting; contemplating; and looking deep inside yourself for your biases, hidden agendas, and memory Xs and triggers that could be clouding your judgement and creating blind spots in your leadership.

It's difficult, but if you use the power of team, you can make the journey with success. In my own life, I often use my team to help navigate me back to Quadrant 2. The best example is my wife and business partner, Karen, who is able to shift my focus in a nanosecond from Quadrant 1, "lost in technical details" afternoon or a Quadrant 4 "all about me" behavior to Quadrant 2. I can even be in the middle of a Quadrant 1 or 4 "adrenaline-sponsored" international keynote address, and with one small hand gesture Karen can stop me in my tracks and positively change the entire outcome.

She has developed a whole playbook of signals just like a skilled third base coach in professional baseball. My favorite is the index finger to the nose. When she gives me this signal it means I'm losing the crowd because of a Quadrant 4 lack of situational awareness. When I see the signal, I stop, even if I'm halfway through a story, re-calibrate my brain to Quadrant 2 – all the while letting the audience know exactly what is happening – apologize if appropriate and then merge back into the talk. It is transformational for me and for the room. If you ever get a chance to take in one of my speaking engagements and Karen is in the room, get your full money's worth and set yourself up so you can see the stage and observe Karen at the same time.

As a leader you stand many times at this crossroads. Do you lose the room in technical jargon or in self-centered ego and agenda, or are you committed enough to Q2 outcomes to stop, breathe, think and change your trajectory? Do you have a trusted person at your meetings who can help you? It could be a VP or your Executive Assistant. CEOs need people to keep them in Quadrant 2 so they can stay committed to the journey of transformation.

Achievement targets are massively important, and when you combine them with transformational targets, you have a fully switched-on system. I'm connected to a CEO who illustrated this switched-on approach perfectly. The CEO was new to the position, and had the task of turning the company around. The board was focused on the journey of achievement – becoming profitable – and the CEO, aware that time was of essence, knew he needed to leverage a "Switched-On" approach. This meant including both the journey of achievement and the journey of transformation.

Early into his new role, the CEO was talking with one of his key leaders when a female employee walked by. Mid-conversation with the CEO, this key leader broke his focus to watch the woman walk down the hall. When he regained his focus the CEO simply told the key leader that behaviour like he just demonstrated had to stop. "Under my leadership," the CEO stated, "we will respect, honor, trust, and build safety for all we come into contact with." This micro-transformational conversation about values will not make it onto the performance evaluation, but combined with achievement targets it creates a gold standard for leadership.

It is often easy to determine a very basic, linear, way of reaching your achievement targets. You can measure them and gauge your progress. When it comes to transformational goals, however, these are best reached by setting intentions.

We all have intentions every day. When we can consciously set an intention to attain something, it makes reaching the actual target more realistic. Think of it this way: achievement targets are like setting "IQ" intentions and transformational targets are like setting "EQ" intentions. For instance, if you set the intention to be less reactive in high-pressure situations as a transformational goal, charting your progress becomes an exploratory process as you work your way through the Switchback diagrams, talking to peers, seeking out experts, finding and learning from mentors. It doesn't come to you all at once. The brain has built its operating system around its current stimulus; shifting a core belief, or, in this example, a core character trait, takes time.

SETTING INTENTIONS

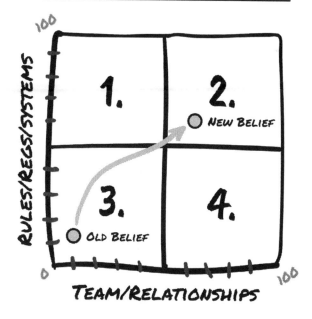

Once you set your intentions, think about them on a daily basis. Identify three or four intentions you have for work, home, or your community. Don't overload yourself with intentions, though, because this is truly foundational work. Most people think that EQ goals are impossible, that the brain is hard-wired and the formation of new beliefs is unrealistic. For you to be working on three intentions is already huge to begin with.

Plot out what you want to work on at the transformational level, and then decide where the easiest place will be to measure the impact. Is it at work? At home? In the community? They're all going to be affected anyway, so find the most impactful place where you can measure your progress. Choose a time in the day when you have five or ten minutes of calm in your mind to remind yourself on a daily basis what your intentions are.

It's really as basic as that. It's amazing how your brain will work for you for free, if you set a target, aim high with what you imagine to be the possibilities, and then you set your intentions. If this feels a little bit outside of the wheelhouse of your daily life, I encourage you to try it anyway. It's a game-changer.

Chapter 7

The Six Profiles

SWITCHBACK'S SIX PROFILES OFFERS YOU A CHANCE to step back and do a new form of analysis based on the paradigm of Switchback thinking. These profiles come into play when we think and act outside of TEAM and self-sabotage ourselves and each other. The profiles are called: Passive Asset, Big Bill, Captain Rejection, Troll, Cave Dweller, Snowball Throwers. I'm sure just from the names you already have an idea of what thinking and behaviors these profiles represent.

So, what is the manifestation of a Snowball Thrower? What is the manifestation of a Cave Dweller, a Troll, a Captain Rejection, a Passive Asset, or a Big Bill? Is it their personality? Or is it more complex? The Switchback answer is the latter. The six profiles are the reactive coping response of people, groups and systems when they exit team, either on their own volition or by being pushed out by systems or by other people.

If a CEO is honest and able to look both backwards and broadly, they will most likely find personal examples of manifesting all six profiles. Switchback's new benchmark for CEOs is to be able to perform day in and day out within Quadrant 2 and within the TEAM/SUCCESS zone of the front of the brain. This gives the CEO the greatest chance of maintaining the right, the moral authority, to lead.

In the past, profiling was seen as a personality discovery tool. Switchback uses the 6 Profiles as a way of defining behaviors that demonstrate negative coping, outside of team, or reactive escaping. The behaviors need to be acknowledged, understood (both history and current situation), brought into control, and transformed.

The 6 Profiles work as an early warning system. The CEO might be in a meeting when a thought crosses her mind. She might think, "That sounds like Captain Rejection," so she'll stop, think, talk it out (internally or externally), re-calibrate, and re-message. This way she's putting the front of her brain in charge of thoughts, actions and outcomes. The profiles are exaggerated, unvetted, unreliable reactions to current stimulus supported by memories that haven't yet been processed by the front of the brain.

I believe that personality profiling is non-productive, unhealthy, and often creates silos and echo chambers, not teams. Words are nuclear. Words confine people. Words label people. Words limit people's ability to achieve greatness. The world of personality profiling is full of words that do not build life or capacity, but rather constrict. They create opportunities for people to self-defer, to check out of healthy team, and to hide behind a label.

Take something as basic as the DOPE Bird Personality Test. In this personality test, we have owls, eagles, peacocks, and doves. Right away you know what they all are. The owls are the wise introverts, the eagles are the type A personalities, the peacocks are the extroverts, and the doves are the peacemakers. What is the value of having your executive team go through this exercise of labeling each other?

Everyone at the leaders' table thinks the last thing they want to be is a dove, so now they're all eagles. The accounting department thinks they're smarter, so they're the owls. The sales guy knows he's the only one not terrified of public speaking, so he's the peacock. Someone in HR who took a course in mediation decides, okay, she's the dove. Now you've stratified your senior leadership. What is the value of that exercise? How has it helped you build team? You may believe that it helps people pinpoint and work within their strengths. I challenge that idea, because if I was only working within my strengths my back of the brain spelling problems would have sabotoged my efforts to write a book and I would not be writing a business book today. I would be working at a job that didn't require reading and writing. I would probably be miserable because I was called a gifted and talented underachiever due to some serious issues around my ability to comprehend and learn which were changeable back brain issues.

It would be lovely if we could all work towards our strengths, but the CEO position is typically not working towards the strengths that got you to that job. The strengths that got you to the job were most likely related to fantastic technical execution. This made you an expert in your field. You are now a generalist leading the troops, and your primary job is to build trust at every level so people maintain open communication with each other, so the experts get along with each other, and so things take place in a timely manner. That is not the skill set that you necessarily needed to achieve your earlier results.

As a result, if you are a driven eagle, and you take your eagle into the C-suite, are you going to drive people into team or out of team? On the Switchback diagram, it would show you're being way too aggressive. An eagle model is not appropriate or healthy for a CEO.

Let's say you came through sales and marketing because you were an international genius at getting million-dollar contracts with your products in Asia. Now you're in the C-suite and, boy, you are really good at customer acquisition, but you are terrible at complex project management. All talk, no action: the peacock. This is not an appropriate role to try to play out as a strength. If you're a peacock CEO, people are going to think of you as arrogant – all talk and no substance. They're going to think you're over-promising and under-delivering. You will cut your own feathers right off with your own words three months into the job, if you're a peacock. That is not an acceptable personality profile for a CEO.

How about the owl? You come through finance and legal and no one can find a single mistake in your financial reports. You pride yourself in your work. Now you are the CEO, and you're a generalist. You're dealing with unions, environmental blockades, and people, people, and more people and you can't create perfection for any of those spots. If you approach the CEO role as an owl, you will be featherless because you will pull them out one by one out of frustration and anxiety. You will be a naked owl hovering in your little tiny nest with the office door barricaded, as miserable as you've ever been in your life.

You cannot be a successful CEO as an owl, nor can you be as the dove. The dove is the peacemaker, the one who builds social goodwill. What a lovely role to play out if you are the ability manager within your company, or the campus recruiter for new engineers to your firm, because in a role like that you need to be warm, loving, caring, and empathetic. As a dove CEO, you're going to be seen as the biggest pushover in the C-suite. The eagles are going to have you for breakfast. The peacocks will tell you lies, and the owls will not respect or trust you.

From my point of view, you don't want to be any of these profiles. What you want to be is a mentally tough, fully engaged, front-of-the-brain leader who has the capacity to lead the company with the wisdom of an owl, the drive of an eagle, the inspiration of a peacock, and the loving care of a dove. You need all those characteristics manifested at the right times within the targets that we've set out if you want to be an effective CEO. This translates to being an effective parent, an effective kids' coach in minor sports, and an effective volunteer in the community.

The day and age of personality profiling has got to end. I wish they would dig a hole and bury these profiles. It is time for neuroplasticity to win out over labels and words that actually drive people out of team and into unhealthy styles of leadership that are off-center.

After years of personality profiling, the primary benefit to the CEO of the 6 Profiles we use in Switchback is to introduce a new way of working with people's thoughts and behaviors that is not as limiting as personality profiling. The CEO now has new language to use when he needs to bring people back into team. He might now say things like, "To me, your last verbal outburst started out as a Big Bill, then landed on some unresolved Xs, and quickly turned into a snowball war. I think I speak for the room: we are very interested in what your front brain wants to say. Take a step back and please try again, this time in TEAM."

Having a common language for the thinking and behavior not only makes it easier to call out people in terms of verbiage, but it also leaves no doubt as to how that person's reaction has been received. After only three days of Switchback training, I've heard CEOs call their team back using this language. It sounds like this:

"In the last 30 minutes some of you have slipped out of team. Some I suspect are still front-brain passive but I can tell by some of your expressions and body language that a number of you have picked up Xs and are now hamster-wheeling on Captain Rejection thoughts or, worse yet, right now hiding out in caves. I speak on behalf of those who have put their trust and employment into our hands: we need you to engage. We need your thoughts, your ideas and your input. I'm going to call a 10-minute break. During the break, reach out to your support folks, family or trusted colleague and do what you need to do to get your brains back into team. I will check in around the table when we reconvene to both confirm that we are in team and to collect some of your front brain thoughts on the previous discussion."

Yes, it's totally possible! So what exactly are these profiles?

THE 6 PROFILES

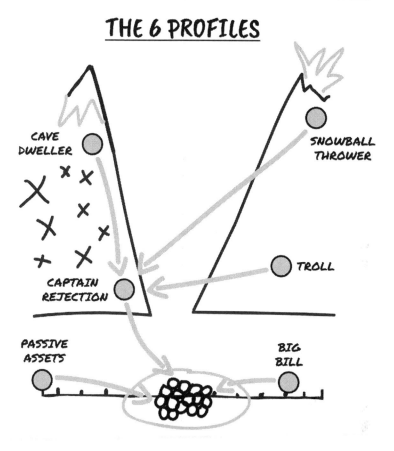

Have you already met Big Bill? Big Bill is all ego. Opposite to Big Bill is Passive Assets, great thinkers but not able or willing to contribute. Then there's Captain Rejection. She views her world through a lens of low-level rejection. Then there are Trolls, and all they do is blame others and speak negatively. Next are the Cave Dwellers, who are isolated and think that isolation is safe and secure. Cave Dwellers can be found hiding in any organization. They have locked themselves into a cubicle and their goal is not to be noticed. They go through a very lonely existence. Up on that snow-capped flight mountain you die of hypothermia. It's cold, it's lonely and it's a hostile, dangerous existence.

Finally, there are the Snowball Throwers. They could be called bullies but we're using new words in Switchback. These employees throw snowballs at the leaders who are trying to build team. They also pick on the Cave Dwellers. This is a serious issue in the workplace. Sometimes the Cave Dwellers convert to Snowball Throwers and become gang members because it's better to join the bully than to be bullied.

As I mentioned earlier, these are not personality profiles. These are just places where you can end up and, unfortunately, it's due to stimulus. Confession: I've been all six of these characters – and chances are, so have you. In different circumstances and at different times you can find yourself being passive and not speaking up when you should, or you find yourself being like Big Bill, thinking that you know all the answers, exaggerating or bragging over talking. You might have a Captain Rejection moment, where you think nothing will ever work.

Sometimes, while driving or before sleep comes, leaders slip into Captain Rejection thinking patterns. You may have had your own moment in the cave when you felt like giving up, or even a moment as a Snowball Thrower, where you rained on someone's parade. In our training, we have people self-identify. After the training, and with implementation over time, the 6 Profiles become buzzwords within the culture of the company. At a managers' meeting you might hear someone say, "Whoa! Did you just chuck a snowball at me?" They'll say. "Yeah." Another leader will chime in, "Well, you must have hit an X! What was it?" They use this language on a day to day basis. A common language is powerful.

Using these profiles is another tool for your toolkit when you need to bring people back to team. Remember, the power of success is in team. For a good CEO, attuning to people's thoughts and behaviors becomes an innate ability, and will always help you get your team on track. Here are some exercises to get you started.

Exercises:

Privately draw out the 6 profiles on the Switchback Brain diagram. Add six people whom you know, one for each profile, who are currently stuck in the profile. People can get stuck when they spend too much time in one behavior, because the brain is like a muscle. Whatever you exercise gets stronger and whatever you don't exercise become weaker. As you repeatedly use a certain neurological pathway it becomes the preferred response.

Now build a plan that would help a friend or co-worker unhook from the profile you see them in and work their way down the mountains and from the outer edges of the front of the brain into team. What would it take? What would your strategy be?

Have your leadership team list all six profiles in order of most used to least used. Analyze your lists as a team.

For CEOs: have the executive team identify employees, stakeholders and/or contractors who are stuck in each of the profiles. Build a timeline and a plan to bring each one back into team.

Chapter 8

The 3-Lane Highway
of Communication

COMMUNICATION IS MORE COMPLEX THAN WE
often realize. I watch people struggle to communicate
all the time. I watch people struggle in the boardroom, I
watch supervisors struggle to communicate something
as fundamental as a safety briefing, I watch new and
young workers struggle on a basic level in conversation
with their supervisors on the foundational instructions
for their day-to-day activities, and I watch boards of
directors engage and disengage in often arrogant ways
that are just not appropriate.

If we observe this struggle and match it to the human
condition, we might find ourselves wondering if these
people are doing it on purpose. Is it a learned behavior? Is this personality-driven? What is negotiable here?
Regardless of what we determine to be the cause, the

truth is that people can change thanks to neuroplasticity. I have a really strong hunch that people communicate poorly not because that's what they want, but because they don't understand the complexity of what's going on.

Part of Switchback's gift to CEOs, the business world, and government is to lay out a very simple yet profound playbook for healthy, functional communication. Over my years as a family therapist, it became clear that people were discovering and developing a great deal around neuro-programming and neural pathways. The question they were asking revolved around identifying the place of change. Is it within the system? The individual? The community? The answer is that change needs to operate in all three. Even beyond that, we can say the place of change happens in metacognition, in our unspoken and unexpressed thoughts.

Here is our basic game plan for communication: If you want to become a world-class communicator, become willing and able to stop and think. Think about your thoughts. Find your Xs and move them. Be willing to analyze what just happened, and be able and willing to analyze it on a level of honesty and transparency to yourself, so that you can actually understand and learn from it.

It helps to become able to observe others and not just assume that if a person is funny, they've always been funny, because it's not true. People develop skills and then they're encouraged in these skills. You can become a student of human behavior, and doing so you make every hour of your day, every executive team meeting so much more interesting.

Communication is an internal process. It's a personal process, a group process and a larger system process. The more you make this one of your priorities of study, the more you'll gain huge benefit from tools like Switchback. At the end of the day, companies and leaders that communicate effectively are the ones that experience long term sustainable success, and not just success at work, but success at home and in the community as well.

The old way of doings things was to compartmentalize, and this was exacerbated by how people communicated. Work, home, community were all kept separate. While some systems still model this world view (for example military training) what happens in Vegas no longer stays in Vegas, especially as a lot of it is now seen on social media. The compartmentalized world, the one where no one from the office even knew you had a cocker spaniel or that you liked to knit, is gone. It doesn't exist in today's world, and because of this we have to be more integrated, thoughtful and mentally tough. We have to change; we have to find a new target (Quadrant 2) and then make this the goal for all aspects of life – home, work, community. We have to harvest our Xs because they're going to come back to bite us if we don't. And when they do, someone will post a picture of it.

This is especially true for business leaders. The way we manage in this world of de-compartmentalization and open-source living is by developing this capacity. Think back to one of the favorite bosses you've ever had. You knew that boss cared. That boss was interested enough to care about your Cocker spaniel. It's as simple as offering a point of deeper connection two or three comments into your conversation.

Leave the Warrior Culture Behind

While compartments are being broken down, we're also seeing more workplaces that are really like war zones. Teams are overworked, the communication stream of emails is endless and the whole system is tiring. Fatigue occurs for everyone on the team, including the leader. It's collateral damage, an "incident within an incident." When leaders get tired you don't recognize that you're in a war zone, but it's exactly the warrior culture that's making you tired. You might try to medicate your symptoms, which is how you can end up disgruntled and overweight. But what if you could leave the war zone behind and change everything? What if you could do that by establishing a new approach to communication?

Just as lead and lag indicators are found in the business community, lead and lag indicators are found in your body, in your relationships and in how you respond to stress. Part of being a world-class leader is being able to lead your corporation away from warrior culture into something that's more sustainable, something that's more reasonable. Something that has work-life balance. Companies that can achieve this improve their bottom line every time.

It may sound counter-intuitive, but if you can create a model where everybody, on a consistent basis, leaves work at the end of the day with a quarter tank of gas left in their souls, you've built a perpetual motion machine. Doing this, are you going to attract talent to your company? Are you going to attract loyalty? Are you going to build trust? Of course you will, because people are going to have the sense that they are happy. If they can hit their Friday night with a quarter tank of gas in their tank, why wouldn't that be a credible, measurable goal to try to achieve?

Often, what we experience when we first walk into the companies we work with is a warrior culture: people are on empty, running on fumes. They've gotten good at it, and that's the crazy part about it. Not only have they gotten good at it: it has become the expectation. As a result, you as CEO also have no gas left at the end of the day and for the weekend, and so the temptation is to medicate the problem using false fuel types in an attempt to fill the tank.

Worse than medicating is when, if you're really working in a warrior culture, you find comfort in being *outside* of the team. You go into passivity or you become angry, aggressive, curt. You might be short-tempered with your kids; you've had a stressful day and now because of the war zone at work you choose to spend your first hour with your kids by barking at them. Part of your brain knows it makes no rational sense, but you're caught. This is one way warrior culture spills out and impacts those around you. Even worse, you might end up rejecting your family altogether and not even coming home; you go to the gym to avoid dealing with the kids. You've pushed yourself right out of team. Is this what you really want? Of course not!

What we've found is that, with a simple switch to how you approach communication, you can powerfully shift the culture at work. You can become the CEO who cares, and is metric-driven at the same time, tending to the x and y axes of the 4 Quadrants.

We've taken the basics of everyday communication and made it even easier for anyone to move to meaningful connection in a few short sentences. We call it the 3-Lane Highway, where Lane 1 is small talk, Lane 2 is information, and Lane 3 is reserved for significant critical human connection.

How it Works

The 3-Lane Highway is the communication tool we use in Switchback. I came up with it to counter what I was seeing; communication techniques and tools are notorious for being mechanical, oversimplified and easy to spot in a conversation. Just think back to the last sales presentation you heard and how it was so easy to hear the script behind the pitch.

Switchback's communication tool needed to be more flexible and natural while maintaining a measurable structure. It also had to be as effective on a date or when talking with small children as it would be in a board meeting. Today, for tools to be embedded, sustained and integrated into the DNA of a company, the tool needs to have high levels of personal benefit. People tell us that they use the 4 Quadrants or Memory Xs or the 3-Lane Highway absolutely every day of their lives, mostly at home. The value and benefit to the company culture to have employees embed tools from work at home is priceless.

The 3-Lane Highway is the simple, measurable tool we use to help teams build communication awareness skills. The basic premise behind the 3-Lane Highway is that it's a tool to merge you into people's lives. What makes it effective is that this can happen in seconds; Even critical conversations can happen in under five minutes.

The initial merge in Lane 1 might be eye contact or a handshake. It could be a simple "Good morning," or a little chat about the weather. It's an opening, and people often don't respect the need for openings. It's a basic people skill, however. Neglecting this or not even noticing this is natural to the flow of conversation means the person is not tracking towards world-class. If you think you're too busy to actually have an opening, and you go right to what we call Lane 2, which is operational conversation, you've instantly lost your chance at connection. It's the difference between this:

> Susan, CEO, encounters Dan from marketing at the water cooler.
>
> **Susan:** Dan! Did you happen to review those notes I sent yesterday?
>
> **Dan:** (surprised) Um. Not yet? (blushes, sheepish – he's busted.)

... and this:

> **Susan:** Hi Dan! How are you?
>
> **Dan:** I'm well, thanks. How are you?
>
> **Susan:** Things are good. Did you catch the hockey game last night?
>
> **Dan:** Sure did.
>
> **Susan:** Yesterday I sent you notes to review on the Simmons project. When do you think you can respond?
>
> **Dan:** Sure. How about in an hour?
>
> **Susan:** Thanks. That would be perfect.
>
> **Dan:** Have a good day.
>
> **Susan:** You, too.

As you can see, opening with small talk allowed Dan to feel a lot calmer about giving Susan an update on the notes. In the first example, when Susan went straight to Lane 2, Dan was blindsided and ended up in the back of his brain. In the second version, not only did Susan slow down by asking Dan how he was, she also connected through something as common as sports. In just this extra bit of time alone, she's got Dan in a much more productive thinking place, and was able to get the info needed on time and more than likely of better quality.

THE 3 LANE HIGHWAY

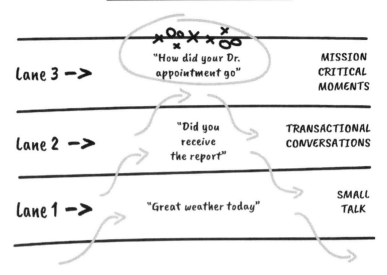

Lane 3 —>   "How did your Dr. appointment go"   MISSION CRITICAL MOMENTS

Lane 2 —>   "Did you receive the report"   TRANSACTIONAL CONVERSATIONS

Lane 1 —>   "Great weather today"   SMALL TALK

I wish I could say there were more CEOs like Susan, but unfortunately, I can't. Many CEOs have read so many time management books that they don't value Lane 1 any more. They skip Lane 1 completely and move immediately to making a Lane 2 request or comment, which is strictly operational.

Some people might think the CEO is a champ for being so professional; others might think it's strange. After all, we are all human, we all have lives and things going on, and even if we didn't watch the "game" the night before, chances are there are events around us that can really help build basic connections.

It's as simple as this: Lane 1, build a connection; it's the tension breaker, it's where humor can play a key role. Lane 2 gets your operational agenda out. Lane 3 conversations are deeper; this lane is for topics that require trust. They also require being attuned to time, place, and person. You can't just run into Lane 3 – especially in a work environment – without being in tune. A lot of people don't have the capacity for the 3-Lane Highway because they are not aware of the need and therefore lack the skill to be able to engage in a Lane 3 conversation.

So Lane 1 is easy – a simple acknowledgment, greeting, small talk. Lane 2 is also easy; it's the standard day to day operational business. Now let's say you have an extra three minutes, and you're trying to build capacity with key people whom you have identified in your log. When there's this window of time and opportunity, watch for the ticket telling you we can go to that next lane. By ticket, I mean a verbal or non-verbal clue that people give out, consciously or unconsciously. If you ask why in a respectful way, even if it takes a few times, you will eventually get to the core of the reason why. When you ask the question why, you're trying to merge into Lane 3. The tickets go both ways; you can offer a ticket and a ticket can be presented to you from others.

So you have asked why. Your ticket is now waiting for the response. After you have offered a ticket, pause and watch the person's demeanor carefully. We're watching for all the conscious, unconscious, verbal, and nonverbal clues. They will give you a yes, no, or maybe depending upon their level of comfort in communicating with you. These are clear responses: "yes" means they're willing; "maybe" means thanks for asking, but they'll get back to you; and "no" means they're not comfortable at that moment. They are unwilling to have this conversation with you right now.

The no is usually a nonverbal, unconscious no. If they're uncomfortable, there is nothing wrong with that. There might be a dozen different reasons why they're not comfortable: because you're standing in the lobby, because you're a male and they're a female, because they haven't processed something with their core people, because they're new to the company. When you hear or perceive "not comfortable", see this as positive, or neutral; don't write it off as negative. Just hold the space.

After receiving the response, you can potentially carry on, or you can hold the space by staying present and allowing the person to gather their thoughts. If they repeat the question back to you or begin to expand on the topic, now you're in Lane 3. You have received their ticket, and the permission to be in this space with that person.

Let's see how Susan might do this with Dan. Now that she's made some Lane 2 conversation and gotten a ticket from Dan, let's see how she moves into Lane 3:

Susan: Okay, I'll be up in about an hour to go over those notes with you. (pause) By the way, how is your son? I hope he's feeling better now.

Dan: Yeah, he is, thanks for asking. The surgery went as good as could be expected and he's already asking when he can get back to playing sports.

Susan: That's great. I'm glad to hear it. I hope he gets to play again soon! (checks her watch) OK, Dan, see you again in an hour.

Susan merged into Lane 3 with the question about Dan's son, and moved back to Lane 2 when she reiterated their appointment. In her last statement, Susan is beginning to transition out. Dan, meanwhile, feels seen and supported. He knows that Susan is aware that things have been stressful for Dan at home. Susan took a risk to ask about his injured child – his surgery could have gone horribly wrong. He may have been told he'll never play sports again. She could have opened up a big can of worms. Still, she took the risk, because even if she "overstepped" into Dan's family life there's always a measure of respect for taking a risk if you do it right.

How long did it take for Susan to get into Lane 3? Not very long. The question you always want to keep in mind throughout the process is this: are you developing team? In this case, Susan was developing team because Dan sensed that empathetic connection between himself and Susan, and now the work is done.

There is a basic human need, to be known. This need is amplified with our relationships with authority figures. We want to be seen and known by the boss.

On every single level, when approaching communication this way, you are meeting a basic human need. You are stopping and seeing the person. That person is visible to their authority figure. Wouldn't your office and your organization love to know that they are visible to you and that you are visible and available to them, not just when there's a crisis or fatality, but because of your company culture?

This is what our 3-Lane Highway approach is about; building capacity around your team so you can gauge your ability to connect with people. You can then take this technique and apply it throughout your life. It works really well when you apply it to your family life.

I was on the road with Switchback and we taught the 3-Lane Highway communication tool during our Three Day Foundation Training session. The VP of an energy company was a confident self-made leader who through the course of the training talked about how over the past 15 years he had lost TEAM with his adult son. They just couldn't navigate a conversation any more without negative consequences. As a result they rarely spoke, and when they did they typically ended the call with both being angry and blowing up at each other.

This VP looked at our Switchback thinking and tools and applied them to how he was communicating with his son. He saw that he was coming in way too aggressively whenever he spoke to his son, and he was doing so because he felt an adrenaline rise just before the communication started. It would only take a few minutes into the conversation before his son would hit one of his Xs or he would hit one of his son's Xs, which switched the conversation into a barrage and counter-attack of unhappy and cruel words. Inevitably, they'd slam the phones down. Classic back of the brain flight /fight reactions.

Because the VP had talked this dynamic out within the Switchback sessions, he leveraged the power of TEAM and was able to capture the complexities of his relationship with his son with the front of his brain. He pieced together a new strategy. Shortly after the sessions, he picked up the phone and called his son. He left a Lane 1 message, commenting on the weather where his son lived and adding a Lane 2 ticket. Click. Then he waited. Within five minutes, the phone rang. The VP picked up the phone, heart thumping hands sweating, and it was his son. They started riding down Lane 1 and naturally bumped over to Lane 2. So far so good. Metacognition (thinking about his thoughts) was in full gear.

Then the conversation shifted into Lane 3. They had entered the danger land, littered with memory Xs for both of them. It would have been easy to fall into the old traps, —land on Xs, overreact, and hang up the phone angry. But this VP had spent three full training days with us, and he knew about building team by finding the gold in their lives – shared, happy moments. In this case, he had golden memories of his son from back in the days when they used to surf together.

While in Lane 3, the VP shifted the conversation toward the gold, the things held as sacred in both of their lives. He recounted some of these memories to his son: the setting sun, the perfect curl, the wave action, the feeling of being free and alive, loving each other and loving life. He just went there, knowing that Lane 3 also stored their relational Xs. He managed to hold the conversation in Lane 3 for just the right length of time – too much longer and he would have risked increasing the intensity of the conversation to the point where he or his son might lose front brain command and switch back into Xs.

Interestingly, his son did verbalize a couple of Xs while they were in Lane 3. But this time, instead of the dad reacting with his own Xs, he made a mental note to remember the Xs for another time and didn't take the back-of-the-brain bait.

They wrapped up the memories of surfing, and merged cleanly back to Lane 2 and then Lane 1, talking about the weather. They then said goodbye and hung up.

He did it. He broke the pattern of pain and disfunction with his son. After this, the VP was on fire, he had to tell someone. He burst into the office next door, "guess what I just did!" Tell me that wasn't the highlight of his month, or his quarter. We were in an after-action debrief session a couple of offices down the hall, had the privilege of hearing his story and celebrating with him.

This is the power of the 3-Lane Highway, and it's amazing how effective it is, wherever you apply it. Now that we've gone through the 3-Lane communication highway in a general way that can be used in the workplace, in the next chapter we'll look at how it translates into working with the full team, at a meeting, for example, and dive deeper into understanding what you as CEO can focus on when applying the Switchback System.

Chapter 9

The -3-Lane Meeting

IT'S ONE THING TO USE THE 3-LANE HIGHWAY communication method in a one-on-one situation, but what
about when you're addressing a group of people? Let's
imagine a typical event in the daily life of virtually any
company: a meeting.

Usually at the start of a meeting, the CEO gives a
greeting or welcome message. They will walk through
the room in a warm, affirming way, peppering the room
with comments like, "Glad you made it," and "Nice to
see you," along with, "Thanks for setting up the room"
etc. Then they give the invitation to get started.

As the CEO takes their place at the front of the room,
they start with Lane 2 conversation comments around
the logistics of the meeting, the length it is planned for,
and the agenda. Let's imagine that this meeting has four
items on the agenda: 1) production forecast, 2) project
management plan update for new product line, 3) harass-
ment allegations at operation X and 4) safety report.

While the meeting may stay in Lane 2 for a while, eventually the CEO will take it into Lane 3. If you look at the agenda items, item three is both a Lane 2 and a Lane 3 topic. It's operational at one level, but once discussion begins on the topic it will become obvious that this topic is deeply impactful in a human way, which makes it Lane 3.

If you were the CEO for this meeting, how would you handle this? Would you keep things in Lane 1 for as long as possible? Would you go right into that Lane 3 conversation, no holds barred? As the CEO, you will gain a deeper level of respect and status if you are perceived as a leader who can take a room in and out of all three lanes with ease, grace, and professionalism. Your team will trust you and honor your role while seeking ways to maintain loyalty.

Taking yourself too seriously all the time is actually bad for your company culture. Knowing and valuing the communicators on your team who can transition the room from heavy to light is critically important. It follows that becoming skilled yourself at making a lane change from Lane 3 to Lane 1 at exactly the right time is extremely valuable.

As for those Lane 2 conversations, Lane 2 skills are what helped you climb to your current position of leadership, but they are now left for others. At most, you will facilitate Lane 2 conversations. Let others lead and take operational responsibility.

Your role is to inspire (Lane 3), heal (Lane 3), console (Lane 3), coach (Lane 3), and hold people deeply accountable (Lane 3). Your role is also to warm up the room (Lane 1), help people relax (Lane 1), and get laughter rolling as healthy chapter breaks between items (Lane 1).

Avoid the T-Bone Crash

Without accruing some skill in how to ride the 3-Lane Highway, there is potential for you to use this tool ineffectively, in both a passive and an aggressive way. The aggressive approach to using the 3-Lane Highway tool looks like t-boning the situation, taking the conversation straight to Lane 3 regardless of context.

My friend has a good example of this. He was camping with a few families on a long weekend. As parents they had finally tucked their kids into the tents, which of course was a big ordeal, and they were enjoying the fire. My friend had just sat down beside his wife, when one of their buddies leaned over and asked, "So, when was the last time you and your wife had a really big fight?"

My friend was understandably dumbfounded. Why would somebody ask that question? Who opens with that? Was his buddy in a misplaced career and secretly harboring the desire to be a family therapist? Or was he fighting with his own wife and seeking validation?

Whatever the reasoning, we call that t-boning the 3-Lane Highway. By asking that question – going directly to Lane 3 – this misguided person created a huge crash. He was so eager to get to Lane 3 that he completely bypassed Lanes 1 and 2. If my friend had recently had a big brawl with his wife, of course it would have been awesome to have a trusted person with whom he could debrief. In this case, however, because his buddy t-boned him, my friend actually ended up with a fresh X. His back brain fired up and a new limiting belief arose warning him to be careful, this buddy is not safe.

Some CEOs have become lazy, undisciplined communicators and share this bad habit of t-boning unprepared victims. Due to their position of power, they seem to have lost the social graces of lane changing in the service of ego. It's almost like an overcompensation due to an acute sense of lack. Striking first, keeping people off their balance, is a very unhealthy way to lead.

THE 3 LANE HIGHWAY T-BONE

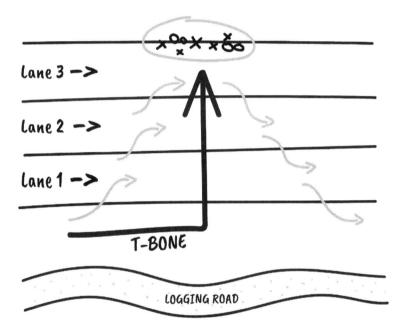

Just like a CEO who insulates because of risk management, we can insulate ourselves in our personal lives. We think maybe it's easier if we talk about other things; if we keep it operational. Think of couples who have been married for fifty, sixty years. So many of them have an operational relationship but not a world-class relationship. If you actually analyze their conversation through the day, they never take a step out of Lane 2 towards Lane 3.

We perceive them as happy and compatible, which they might be, and which is okay—but they're not world-class. When there's a crisis, they can't step up because they haven't developed the capacity to do so. When there's something to celebrate, they don't know how to embrace it because they don't have the capacity. They're stealing from their own lives! They can't celebrate the birth of their great grandkids at an appropriate level. They also can't go to their friend's funeral and really experience that level of humanity.

In the work setting, we've observed that leadership teams that lack the capacity of Lane 3 communication generally struggle to deal with these types of issues and will default to Lane 2 which, in the end, erodes the goodwill of the culture and limits the company's ability to ever become world-class. Teams like this may skip the 3-Lane Highway entirely and take the Logging Road.

The Logging Road

Riding the Logging Road is the passive approach to using the 3-Lane Highway tool.

It's the cop-out communication road. Being on the Logging Road is like eavesdropping on lanes as you cruise on your road beside the team who are riding the 3-Lane Highway. If you're on the Logging Road, you have no skin in the game.

Some CEOs are guilty of this bad communication habit. They "empower others" but really abdicate leadership and then sit back and take no ownership regarding the process, structure, functionality or outcome. It's like a parent calling a family meeting, playing on their phone throughout the meeting, and then blaming the children for inferior outcomes. This is not a leadership style, this is a cop out. If you are copping out, it's up to you to reach out to TEAM and figure out why. Sort out your Xs and limiting beliefs, wash your face, metaphorically speaking, get back in TEAM and get back on the 3-Lane Highway.

THE 3 LANE HIGHWAY WITH LOGGING ROAD

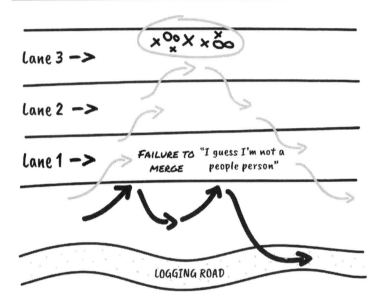

Imagine that, as CEO, you want to engage with your team in accounting. They don't engage. Okay, you think, they're accountants. But wait – is that thought your way of profiling their personalities? So you try again, high-fiving your way through the office. This time they roll their eyes and say nothing, even though they think you're being silly. You try to engage a couple more times and get one, two, three rejections and soon enough, you've got an X in the back of your brain: accountants aren't humans (you say, sounding like a Troll), you're not cut out for this kind of leadership (Capital Rejection) and you ought to stick with the numbers (Quadrant 1).

If you're thinking this way, you're on track to hanging out on the Logging Road. You're going to avoid the 3 Lanes altogether and just hang back. You might even get away with this Logging Road default plan. You've got five years left to retirement, so that's where you go. How peaceful would that be? You trick yourself into disengaging, and you've got good reason to because you've been yelled at by the board of directors. You've had environmentalists campaign outside your office. It's been a war, and you're a bit battle weary. You've got lots of Xs that you haven't moved. You think it might be just fine to get on the Logging Road and coast for a while, so you do that.

Now you're just in your office. You look peaceful, serene, but you haven't said an inspired thing in months. You also haven't held anybody accountable, because some of your executive are also on the five-year retirement plan. You're no longer driving the results. It's as if you have an understanding: you're in your five-year dash for cash. This attitude is reflected all the way to the outer edge of your company where the boots are actually on the ground.

And then your phone rings. There has been a fatality in the warehouse of region 5. Someone ended up getting crushed by a forklift. And you, as CEO have zero capacity to walk through that front door and lead.

First you disengage at work, and then you disengage at home, and from your hobbies and things that you used to be passionate about. You stop going to church or to the cinema, and then you sit. You close your eyes, and that's the end. There's no tomorrow. Alternatively, we know 85-year-olds who still do push-ups – but if you're on the Logging Road, chances are good you're not one of them. You're standing at a crossroads. You have all kinds of excuses to be in the position that you're in.

I'm asking you to choose to switch on again. Return to the 3-Lane Highway and, preferably, engage with your team to build 3-lane capacity. We know that you'll need some tools to get there.

Chapter 10

How to Develop 3-Lane Highway Capacity

AT SWITCHBACK, WE KNOW THAT HAVING THE leadership capacity, understanding, and wisdom to be able to shift a room into and out of lanes is critical for excellence, and we help CEOs expand their communication skills by teaching them how to lead 3 Lane conversations and how to develop Lane 3 capacity.

We offer CEOs the following suggestions to develop this skill:

- Be intentional. Tell the room that the topic is shifting into Lane 3.
- Change your voice tone, posture and where your hands are to signal the change.
- Maintain longer eye contact when connecting with the room.

- Use the power of the pause ("the gap").
- Ask others to weigh in.
- Know when the room has traveled long enough in Lane 3 and shift it back to Lane 2. If you don't, people will start leaving team and you will end up with back-of-the-brain comments and reactions that people will wish later they had not verbalized.
- Mentor your senior leaders in shifting in and out of Lane 3 so that they can also use this skill in group and one-on-one meetings.

While I believe a lot of the items on this list come innately, and particularly to people who already have strong interpersonal skills, not all of them are so simple in practice. You have to draw on some different skills that we don't ordinarily promote when training CEOs; there's a level of attunement and awareness that is essential to really maximizing these aspects.

Be intentional

When I say, "be intentional," I am encouraging you to be open and upfront. Tell the room that the topic is shifting into Lane 3. A lot of leaders think that being covert is being kind, and at Switchback we would say the reverse is true. Being covert creates insecurity and can be seen as underhanded and even manipulative. This is why we say be intentional. Be able to talk, upfront, about the agenda and how you want it to be processed.

When you tell the room that the topic is shifting to Lane 3, you might want to reassure people that you won't stay there for long but that you have to be there for a while. Being open about where the conversation is going is also a way of asking the room to engage at that level. If people are still disengaged or on the Logging Road, there's nothing wrong with stopping the meeting and asking them why. Then, with everyone paying attention, ask people to self-reflect on their level of participation in this Lane 3 conversation and ask them to make the necessary shift to be engaged in the moment. The more intentional you are about bringing the team in close by stating overtly what you need from them, the more engagement you'll have in the room.

Change your voice tone, posture and where your hands are to indicate the change

When we shift from Lanes 1 or 2 to Lane 3, we can use our tone of voice, posture, and body language to signify the shift. Becoming a student of people means that you get to also become a student of yourself, so you can see what kinds of results you create by different presentations. Changing your hand or body position can make a difference.

When I took communication labs in undergrad, they taught that the preferred communication stance was an open posture. That means positioning our bodies so they angle slightly to the other person, looking forward, and with no crossed arms or legs. This is actually not great advice for a leader. Leaders need to leverage their bodies to support the message. At times, the open posture would not match the verbal message.

As a CEO, you have the tremendous opportunity to model a level of freedom in your communication, which means modeling arms crossed, standing behind your chair during a meeting, having a foot out to relax your back, leaning back, laughing loudly, leaning in, being deadly serious, standing up and actually moving to where the person you're talking with is, and putting your hand on their shoulder as you tell the staff you all need to support this department over the next 30 days.

What difference would it make if a CEO actually got up out of her chair, walked around the table and stood beside the head of the department that was under so much pressure and then made the request for support? The fact that she got up out of her chair and moved herself over to that department head is profound. It signifies that the department head is a company asset whom everyone needs to take care of and marks the start of a plan to support that department.

As you become an expert student of human dynamics, this kind of thinking and behavior will become natural. It's natural, but it is also planned. Some people say it won't work for them, it's not their style, they're too uncomfortable. You might feel uncomfortable at first, because you have not yet developed the capacity, the muscle memory, to do this. The first few times you adjust your physical body or adjust your voice tone or the speed or volume of speech intentionally will always feel contrived. There might be some self-doubting chatter in the back of your brain. All I can say is, get used to it. Once you practice this a few times, the back of your brain will lose its ability to interfere with the process, and the front of your brain will be able to use these effective communication and team-building tools. Over time, it will become more and more natural.

People are always watching the CEO to see what is permissible and what is not. Consider something as boring as the F word. In some companies, the F word is completely in bounds at all levels of communication because it has been sanctioned by the CEO. In other companies, the F word is not considered to be standard protocol, and it's used here and there, or some people will say the word, and then apologize for saying it, because it is not sanctioned by the CEO. It's not like the CEO sent out a memo forbidding staff from using the F-word, the CEO is leading by example.

If this were an undergraduate psychology course in communication, we'd be saying develop open posture, learn how to paraphrase, learn how to give people reasonable feedback. This isn't that course, however. You're a CEO. It's a lot more complex than that for you, and the last thing we want you to be is contrived, cheesy or mechanical. We want you to develop a repertoire of conscious and unconscious, verbal and non-verbal, clues that build success within your leadership team.

All of these skills are ultimately transferable to your home life, your work in the community, your volunteerism, and even on your holidays, when you're talking with your tour guide in Athens. This is something you will eventually exercise with ease.

Maintain longer eye contact when connecting with the room

Another aspect of non-verbal communication that is very important and often overlooked is appropriate eye contact. I witness key leaders in meetings not making eye contact with the speakers. You miss out on so much when you just look down look away, doodle on your page, or check your phone.

People explain why they have developed this habit in lots of ways; the most common excuse is that they think they're too intimidating or too magnetic, and by not making eye contact they are giving the room the chance to engage. I have the same issue when working with a client in group training. Wherever I am in the room, people tend to focus their eyes on me. I solve this issue be talking openly about the habit, by actually moving around to a different seat and by teaching the why behind this tendency. I might suggest to the next speaker to try to communicate to the whole room while reporting their results, and even mention my awareness of building connection with whomever is on my extreme left side (my old blind spot). Again, overt versus covert communication will usually win the trust of the room. This method does not work if it involves personal correction in front of peers. In this case, make a note of the incident and then seek out a private audience with the person to protect their status and public reputation.

In this age of mobile devices and excessive screen time, we're actually becoming less and less comfortable using eye contact. To move your company to a world-class organization, you basically have to re-introduce the proper use of eye contact. On the continuum we have at one extreme staring people down, which is inappropriate, and at the other not making any eye contact, which is also inappropriate. There's holding your gaze for too long, there's not holding your gaze, or holding your gaze not long enough. There's looking at one eye, rather than both eyes. Clearly, we need to re-establish the basics of appropriate eye contact.

I've come to understand appropriate eye contact through observing leaders in meetings both large and small. First, understand your audience and be willing and able to adjust to their acceptable levels. Once you understand their standards, engage your eye contact in a way that leads the group towards healthy, appropriate interaction. If they are way too aggressive, demonstrate more reasonable engagement with your eye contact by not matching them with a stare down. If they are too passive, reengage them by drawing them into team through deeper, longer eye contact.

Learn to manage and develop your own level of functional, healthy eye contact. I often speak to the folks on the extreme right and left of the room early into a presentation, tell them they are sitting in my natural blind spots, and let them know I'll try to include them in my vision. This builds awareness, accountability and connection in one simple step.

I also make a point of talking directly to individuals in the room rather than just scanning the crowd. I have witnessed too many CEOs look at their screen with their pretty slides and then fix their eye on the back wall above everyone's head telling their story to the wood paneling. It's tragic and you may not even be aware of the message this lack of eye contact sends to your team, colleagues and, worst yet, your family. The wood paneling on the wall does not need your attention. The people in your life would love your eye contact and attention.

You probably have a preferred style and I encourage you to study it. Study this one thing: how you connect with people through eye contact. Figure out if you are the kind of person who uses a staring technique to intimidate people and have them stand down. Maybe you're an avoider, and you're so lost in your own thoughts that in order to get the technical piece right in your brain you close your eyes.

If you have a level of trust with your peers, tell them you are studying how you make eye contact and ask for their honest feedback. You just want to know where you are on the continuum. Are you too passive? Are you too aggressive? Where do you go when you're upset? Or when you disapprove of things? Rejection thinking, under the Troll Bridge, deep in a cave, up on a cliff or with an arm load of snowballs. Quadrant 1, 4, or 3?

Doing this exercise lets you be more cognizant of your eye contact and make any changes you think will help improve your skills in the area. Now, you can recognize this issue in others and build a level of trust so that they will build capacity similar to yours. Your eye-contact habits are not part of your personality, and are not hard-wired. This is habitual response to stimulus that people can change.

Use the power of the pause ("the gap")

If something happens in a meeting or conversation that triggers the fight/flight response, then you have fired up the back of your brain and this in not helpful. What's interesting about the back of your brain is that your response or reaction from there is out of your cognitive control. You're running on instinct. A stimulus comes at you, a barking dog maybe, and your response is to sweat, and your heart rate speeds up. However, we humans have the extraordinary capacity to choose our response to stimulus. We call it creating the gap. The gap is only operational in the front of the brain; it lives between the stimulus and the response.

THE GAP

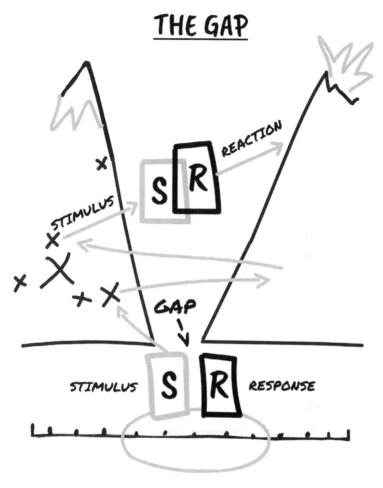

Think about the gap as a micro-second, or one breath. Military people get trained in a breathing exercise called combat breathing, where you breathe through your nose for four seconds, hold the deep breath for seven or eight seconds, and then exhale out through your mouth. This is how sharpshooters make good decisions.

If someone walks towards them looking like a civilian and the rule is they can't shoot civilians (but they know that even someone who looks like a civilian can be wrapped with explosives), they better be practiced and committed to combat breathing. The decision to shoot or not to shoot is accompanied by a lot of back-brain chatter that does not have the advantage of the gap. The front of the brain is about being a professional soldier, who holds another person's life in their hands and remembers the code of conduct for war. When you breathe, you hold that gap, and you stay in the front of your brain.

Take this situation out of a war zone and into the board-room, where this gap is known as the "Boardroom Pause." There's a direct challenge made to you; someone asks you for numbers or something you're not prepared for. You have to stop, apply the gap, take that breath. Ask the question: in light of your history, your current circumstance, and your future goals and dreams, what is the wise thing to do right now? What is the right response?

The right response could only come from the front of the brain, and you need to apply the gap. Stop, breathe, take a drink of water. No one ever criticized people for taking a drink of water. Analyze your thinking, both the back of the brain chatter and the front of the brain pro-cessing. Take another sip of water. Build in more of a gap by acknowledging the question: "Thank you for your question. Please give me a moment."

You could also look up and to the right – another strategy for reducing anxiety and stimulating front brain memory recall. While you are applying the gap, your brain is working at lightning speed and managing the chatter, as well as considering what approach to use to answer the question. If you're still challenged, you can always defer to your team. Table the question by letting people know you're going to consult with your team, the experts, none of whom are in the room. These are the habits of a switched-on CEO. These are the tools that a switched-on organization builds into its culture.

The gap can be as short as a nanosecond and as long as you think is appropriate. In minor hockey coaching classes, we were taught to develop a 24-hour gap any time an upset parent cornered a coach after the game. The script went something like this: "This is an important topic for us to discuss. Can I call you tomorrow around this time when we have both had some time to think it over?" Once you get the hang of it, you'll see how much easier it is to apply the Gap and give yourself and others a moment to Stop and Think.

Taking a pause as you are about to make the shift into Lane 3 is an invaluable practice. In fact, learning to pause, period, will benefit all of your communications. In the US Forest Service Wildland Firefighter culture, they promote a process: stop, think, talk, act. Stopping is the Gap. Especially in the middle of a wildfire, it's vital to Stop. Think, is your plan still current? Has anything changed? Think through your plan, then Talk. Talk it out with your peers and consult the experts. Finally, Act. Act, once you have stopped, thought and talked it through. This process is a powerful re-set to front brain thinking in the heat of the moment.

Ask others to weigh in

The next point is asking others to weigh in. This might seem awkward, but here's the truth of being a CEO: You have now moved into a position where you are no longer the expert. You've spent your whole life being the expert, rising up the corporate ladder, and being the one who has the details within the report. Now you're sitting at the end or the middle of the table, wherever your preference is, and you have 20 expert reports that others have created. Your job is to manage the process and build a level of trust and transparency among your team so that you don't get blindsided when those reports actually get published or executed within the organization.

Asking others to weigh in becomes a critical tool in your toolbox. Here's an example. You're gearing up for a board meeting, and normally you attend these meetings without your senior VPs. However, you know that one of the big issues on the agenda is the environmental impact of operations in Region 3. For this particular topic, an executive of yours is the expert. Why wouldn't you invite your senior executive to that part of the meeting in order to speak to that topic?

You're not abdicating your responsibility. You're actually honoring the expert. You can still take the heat for the results, but there is power in team with this process. Plus, you know what your senior leaders are gunning for. They're gunning for your corner office, so when it's time for you to move on to your next opportunity, or retire, it is a real honor to be able to have one of your VPs chosen as your successor CEO. How is that going to happen, unless you give them the opportunity to experience the world that you work in? They need to be able to operate in the world of stakeholder engagement, dealing with politicians, and dealing with high end regulators, financiers and of course your board of directors? Building the capacity to have people weigh in with you and be the expert is a great tool.

Know the room

Know when the room has traveled long enough in Lane 3, and shift it back to Lane 2 and out to Lane 1 for a break and a breath of fresh air. Actors and performers are trained to merge easily from Lane 1 to 2 to 3 and take the audience with them. We can sense when that shift to something new is coming. Similarly, leaders can apply the same techniques to help a group transition into a new level of conversation. This is why it's so essential for you as the CEO to become aware of and intentional about your tone of voice, and how you use your body and your posture, to create transitions within your meetings.

You can incorporate your body, your position in the room, where you hold your hands, and your full suite of tools in order to transition. It's very powerful, both in board meetings, and when you're out on the road doing town hall meetings with your staff in the different regions.

Let's say you are standing on a podium and talking into a microphone about operational things (Lane 2) and you want to shift your topic to something serious, like safety, because the group you are talking to has experienced a fatality in their operation. In this case, standing behind the podium with the microphone on its stand represents your operational, Lane 2, CEO space. You want to transition the room into another space, so you have to take the microphone off the mic stand and walk to somewhere else, a spot that could be a more sacred space, compared to the operational space.

If I'm doing something like this in a smaller room, I like to grab a chair or a stool and sit down. I wait for the room to become dead quiet, then I choose my tone of voice and pace of speech very carefully as I address the issue. I let the room know that I care and acknowledge that the loss has impacted the operation and community on a deep level. I thank them for being committed to creating a culture where this kind of thing doesn't devastate the community again. Whatever it is that you're discussing, by changing your physical posture or position, your voice tone, tempo and gestures, you're signaling to the group that the topic has shifted.

When you're done connecting in Lane 3, stand up or walk back to the microphone stand, snap the microphone back into place and say, "Now, I need to change topics." The snap of the mic back into its stand lets everyone know that we have changed lanes. Continue with your transition into the Lane 3 gold by highlighting; innovations, accomplishments, hope for the future, the power of TEAM. Then shift into Lane 2 with some operational and corporate information. Finally shift to Lane 1 and end with some kind words. You've just executed a perfect Lane 1, Two, Three, Two, One.

These are points to help you be more effective in navigating your team through all three lanes of communication in a meeting. Now, before I wrap up this chapter, I'd like to address a very common problem that so many companies face: the person in the meeting who talks too much.

The Talking Machine

As the leader you have developed patterns and habits around how you communicate with your people, some of them healthy, some unhealthy. Unhealthy patterns are like letting the people on your team that talk endlessly continue doing so while other team members just sit quietly. This leads the quieter, politer team members to become passive assets and it is already a challenge to get these folks to engage in the discussion. However, outside the room, your passive assets do have opinions which can be of great value. You also may have habits yourself of over-interrupting, over-speaking, being too passive, taking shots over the bow, or dealing with your own insecurities in a way that is not useful. All of this gets formulated into the culture of your executive team meetings.

The 3-Lane Highway and other diagrams can give you and your executive team a fresh chance to reboot your meeting culture. How are you going to do this? By externalizing the Switchback model.

Letting people go on and on and restate their point more than once is one of the worst habits a leader can have when it comes to chairing meetings. Nobody likes over-speakers, I'll be frank. Watch the way your team responds to the over-speaker in your next meeting. When the person starts speaking, they generally get the benefit of the doubt, shown through momentary eye contact from the group. After that, if they are habitual over-speakers, you will notice people slumping their shoulders. They will recline slightly in their chairs. They'll start fidgeting. They'll look away. They will look down. They know that there they are, enduring another monologue for who knows how long.

There's a way for you, as a CEO, to nip that in the bud. First privately coach the over-speaker. Let them know that you are looking for significant change and that you will create systems that will help the whole team function better. As soon as the over-speaker begins, consider interrupting – politely, of course. Just merge in and see if you can encourage the over-speaker to speak to their point for the briefest amount of time possible. Make it a game. Suggest a one minute timer. Once they've agreed on a time, set your timer. Meanwhile, re-engage the rest of the team by inviting them to really be present with what the speaker is saying.

Here's a sample of what you might say:

Oliver Over-speaker: Well, if I may, in this case, the environmental stewardship is in the hands of the company, and we can all do better to improve our systems.

CEO: Excuse me, just a second. I think it's actually really important for all of us to engage on this topic. Can we give this a try? What would be the briefest amount of time you could speak to this topic do you think, and get your point across?

Oliver Over-speaker: Uh, maybe a minute?

CEO: Great. Let's play a little game here. I'll start my timer for a minute, and let's just all, as a room, engage in this really important topic for that minute because, after all, environmental stewardship is one of the tickets that gives us the right to be in business. So for a minute, let's see if we can engage with what you've got to say. Ready? Go ahead.

You've just now created structure, which is the Y-axis. You've created human engagement, which is the X-axis, and a methodology that you can now use to hold everybody accountable to engagement. After the timer goes off, spend a minute go around the room and invite others to use the same minute timer to weigh in. Most of the team is now seeing that this is different. They can't just be fiddling around, thinking about their own presentations or worrying about their unfinished (and overdue) project plan. Now you have a team that is engaged in the present discussion. In short, you've created a Switched-on meeting.

Don't get stuck on the time the speaker takes. Some might think a minute is too short, and others might want three minutes. Setting the timer and putting your phone on the table gamifies the situation. Maybe there are seven of you in the room and you start with the first person, but everyone knows you're coming around to them. You might round out the session by returning to the original speaker to synthesize what they have heard and give everyone a sense of their game plan for the next two weeks. In as little as one minute per person, you have revolutionized your meeting culture.

Be careful of overusing this kind of method, however. It can be seen as a bullying technique, and you'll know when that's happened because you'll notice people disengaging from it. A tool is useful, but only as long as it builds team. The minute the tool stops building team, it's not useful anymore. You have to apply common sense and wisdom when to deploy it.

Some people who are Quadrant 1 might think they are going to apply these tools without using any people skills along with them. They might try to gamify the meeting but they're actually driving their team batty. However, if you use this tool with a level of Quadrant 2 wisdom, you'll realize that it's a neat example of how to revolutionize a meeting using tickets, the 3-Lane Highway, some gamification, and new structure. It's a tool that we will occasionally bring out of our toolbox because it breaks the social norm, which is what is important. It creates an innovative way to build a new level of capacity so that when your team does need to process things quickly, efficiently, and deeply, you have the ability to do it.

It is good to observe how people walk out of the meeting compared to how they walked in. Note their energy levels as they come in. As they proceed through the meeting, check whether people are staying engaged and in the front of their brain, or are slipping into being passive and in the back of their brain. Watch people's micro-expressions as they're leaving the meeting. Are they engaged? Are they full of energy? Does it look like they're running on fumes? Do you know why?

The world is never static. It is continuously dynamic. As a result, as a leader, you are either drawing people into team, or your actions or systems are pushing people out of team.

LEAVING TEAM

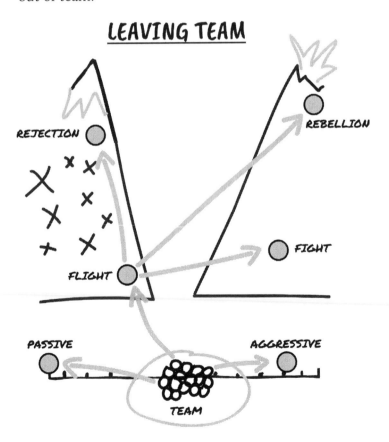

When people leave team, they head towards passivity or aggression, or they will actually leave the front of their brain and head to the flight side of self-rejection thinking. At this crossroad, they have the option of heading into higher level rejection or to the fight side with lower level rebellion or higher-level rebellion.

It's our responsibility as leaders to build a meeting culture that sees people leaving meetings with at minimum half a tank of gas left so they can continue with their day. I'm not saying that we avoid difficult conversations in order to preserve that half tank. I'm saying that there's a world-class Quadrant 2 way to process difficult conversations that actually delivers amazing results and, at the same time, builds resilience in your team.

EXERCISE:

List the top 20 people in your life, including work, home and community.

Check each lane box beside each name if they have Lane 1, 2, 3, capacity.

Then check each lane box beside each name if they have Lane 1, 2, 3 capacity with you.

Interesting observation: As CEOs and parents we get used to expecting others to trust us with their Lane 2 or Lane 3 issues, but do *we* have people in our lives whom we trust with our own Lane 2 or 3 issues? Some CEOs, when pressed, will confess that they have no one that they can currently process Lane 3 issues with. What happens to the Xs that continue to accumulate? What happens to the target of living in Quadrant 2? This little challenge could be the gold you were looking for within these pages. Build your team. Get people in your life with whom you can entrust your Lane 3 issues. The power of success is in TEAM, after all!

Tools for Difficult Conversations

Now you have a Switchback understanding of your brain – and the brains of your employees. You have acquired a new empathy regarding complexity, for yourself and for others, since you know that we're all either reacting to Xs or in the process of moving Xs from back brain unhealthy independence to front brain integration. This will help you be more effective when you meet your employees one on one, whether for plain old conversations or for the difficult conversations that sometimes come up.

Bring that empathy with you now and apply it to your skill working the 3-Lane Highway. Difficult conversations have to happen, and you need to keep in mind that you're going to get triggered, the employee is going to get triggered, and that triggers can happen any time, any place, including something as simple as the conversation moving from Lane 1 to Lane 3 without a ticket.

Imagine one of your VPs is going rogue. You have heard rumblings from the team. Somebody needs to rein this VP in, and guess what? That somebody is you, the CEO. If you're not Switched-On and in the front of your brain in Quadrant Two, you're not going to have that conversation. You're either going to ride this thing out, or build up resentment and end up unconsciously planning the VP's demise, or blowing up in a moment of regrettable back brain fight mountain rebellion. The healthy functional thing to do is have that conversation. Take that step, go through the door, and have it. This is how the 3-Lane Highway can help.

Here's how effectively executing a difficult conversation might look:

CEO: Lane 1: Setting the stage and intentions: I need to have a difficult conversation with you. The topic is insubordination. When is a good time and where is a good place for us to have this conversation?

(get into Lane 2) How about Wednesday? How about 2:00? Let's go to the coffee shop downstairs. Does that sound good?

VP: Yes. Actually, no. Let's do the patio outside our office. That's even better.

CEO: Fantastic. Now, (Lane 3) I'm going to set a 10-minute limit on this conversation, because this is not a conversation we're going to have once. This is a conversation that we need to have on an ongoing basis as we build capacity, because you and I need to rebuild trust and TEAM. It's not going to happen in one shot. So, are we in agreement?

VP: Yes.

CEO: Thank you very much. See you on Wednesday.

On Wednesday, you start in Lane 1. You merge into Lane 2 – order your coffees, check the location. Then, Lane 3, you have the conversation. Then merge back to Lane 2, set up the next appointment. Lane 1, thank you and good bye. It really becomes a pattern, 1-2-3-2-1.

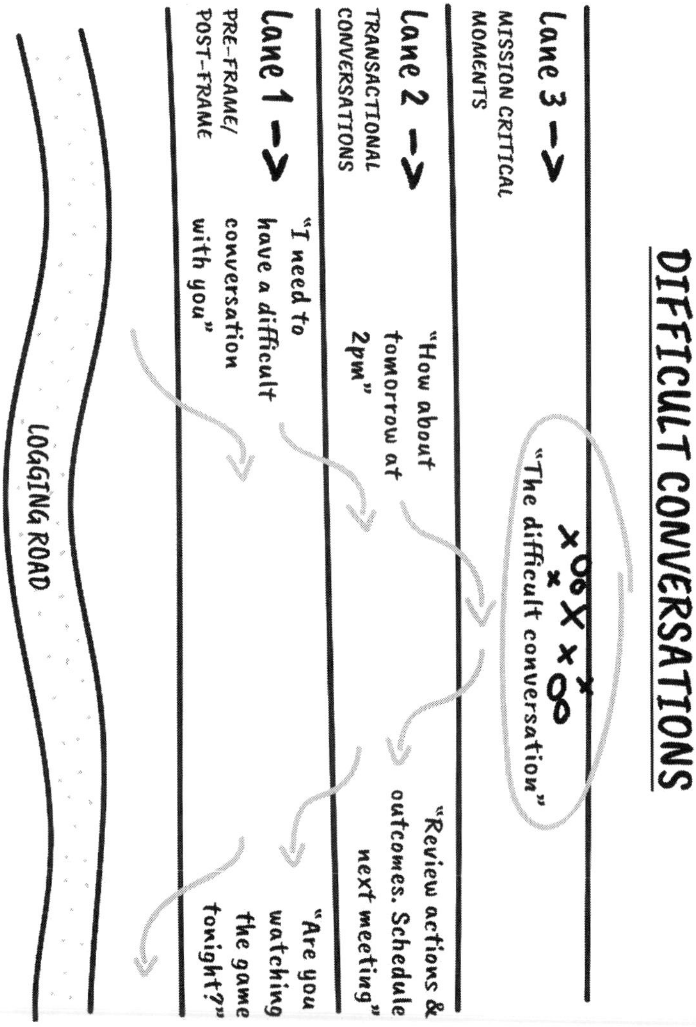

DIFFICULT CONVERSATIONS

Lane 3 →
MISSION CRITICAL MOMENTS
"The difficult conversation"

Lane 2 →
TRANSACTIONAL CONVERSATIONS
"How about tomorrow at 2pm"
"Review actions & outcomes. Schedule next meeting"

Lane 1 →
PRE-FRAME/POST-FRAME
"I need to have a difficult conversation with you"
"Are you watching the game tonight?"

LOGGING ROAD

This is serious, serious business. I encourage you to take notes on the lanes. Lane 1, made contact. Lane 2, set up the time and place. Lane 3, had the conversation. Took notes on the actual conversation. Back down to 2. Set the next appointment, the time and place. Said, "Thank you." That's it.

These logs are helpful, however, as you learn to make this pattern innate. You can add to them what the responses were like, and how your brain responded, both front and back.

Chapter 11

A Winning Team

ALTHOUGH I HAVE ALWAYS BEEN A BUOYANT PER-
son, I too have been through my challenges. A lot of
challenges, really, because I was a gifted and talented
underachiever who felt a deep call in my brain to overcome the underachieving and release the potential of
the gift.

Let's put the process together in an example. Due to
my underachieving in elementary school I stored my success memories in the front of my brain. This supported
my identity as a gifted and talented child. I stored my
memory Xs on the flight mountain at the back of my
brain which supported my underachieving self-rejection
identity.

My Xs were real, not perceived. They were also historical and current. At 44 I was a gifted and talented
underachieving professional who was both brilliant and
painful, world-class and chaotic. By 55 I had leveraged
Switchback thinking and tools. With the strength of

my front brain and the power of TEAM I have treasure hunted my back brain memory Xs and moved them out of independence and into the light. Those that I have uncovered now live healed and resolved in the front of my brain, fully supported by all my success memory storage. This has been a journey of hard work, achievement, and transformational leaps of faith. The underachieving thinking and behaviors have transformed and the gifted and talented truth is now unfettered.

This journey of achievement in academia and business and the equally important journey of transformation, moving Xs challenging and limiting beliefs, and building capacity has renamed my identity as simply 'gifted'. Now I can look out over the blue ocean of opportunity and not trigger the flight-fight response.

I was not solely responsible for this transformation. The power of success is in team. My parents right from the start believed that someday I would overcome my underachieving and shine. When Karen married me, she was taking a risk because the diamond was still in the rough. With her consistent support, we achieved together what would have been impossible for me on my own. Having the department head at graduate school see my gifts and work to "ramp the campus" for me, so the journeys of achievement and transformation could take place, was instrumental. Yes, I forced myself into areas of weakness – and when I did, I was backed up by team almost immediately.

The power of team as a belief really hit home for me in the early days of Switchback. We had just completed our first major project for a large maintenance company in oil and gas. When their positive results started showing up, the parent company that contracts them took notice. They reached out and set up an initial call. Wow, everything was coming into place. Then, on the evening before the big call, it happened. In a moment everything changed.

I was playing ice hockey with my friends at 10:30 pm and lost an edge on my Quadrant 3 skates (my son's old super-expensive skates that had seen better days). As I slid towards the boards I thought I was okay with body position, but my left leg was pitched under my butt. When my skate hit the boards, my ankle shattered into seven pieces and small fragments. More complications followed. I crashed post-surgery because my lungs weren't able to absorb oxygen. I ended up in the intensive care unit for three days.

At the time, our company was at a fragile state where I was the only one to take the call with this critical company. The call was pushed back, and then it never happened. It was as if our future success had been within reach and then disappeared. The window closed.

The combination of pain, medication, and a six-month recovery, with another surgery after the primary surgery, caused me to spiral into a negative place. My life was all about risk and pain management. Anyone who understands chronic pain would have told me it was obvious: it seems like there's no escape from that negative mindset when one is in pain.

Up to that point, however, I would have said that I had the ability to pull myself out of my own cave and even out of Quadrant 3. But there I was. Because Karen was so close to my pain she also didn't have the ability to pull me out of my cave. She was in a similar space. She was wringing her hands, lamenting that the cash flow and bookings had dried up, experiencing stress from all the complexities of running a young business.

Earlier that year I had hired a retired CEO who had been one of the pioneers in the aquaculture sector. He joined us as a part-time employee but really as a mentor. He is amazing. Because he's a switched-on CEO and has a tuned-in intuition, he phoned me and announced he was coming over. He didn't ask; he told. He knew that I needed team and that he could help, and so he came. There I was, lying on the couch in self-pity because it still felt better to have the leg elevated and because I had over the six months created a new identity around the newly formed Xs and limiting beliefs. He came in and drew a chair close to my couch. Then, he just listened. He listened to my operational woes.

He heard all about how we had lost the lead into the next level. He heard all about how some of the team was at that moment sitting in their own homes and not operational. He heard how fragile the company was, and how too much of the company was riding on me. He heard how this was essentially a test of our systems and that our systems were failing because there we were, stalled out as a company. There I was, too, not knowing whether I'd ever walk or run again.

This wise, seasoned leader listened, and gave me a look only a CEO who has been to war and built a sector could give. In a very quiet voice, he said, "Steve, I have no doubt in my mind regarding the long-term success of Switchback."

Neuroplasticity happened in that moment. Something changed in my brain. I could actually feel the sparkle. It was like pixie dust in the air and it caused my brain to reformat itself, not to my limiting beliefs, but to his trust in the long-term success of Switchback.

I got off the couch, reengaged my entrepreneurial brain, moved the X of the injury to the front of my brain, and conquered the limiting beliefs that life was over as I knew it. I rebuilt momentum in the team, picked up the phone and re-engaged with our clients.

Since that moment, I've never looked back. If you're a CEO, a senior leader, a board director, if you just have five years or two levels of greater expertise, or if you're a mom or dad, aunt or uncle, you have the potential to launch this level of profoundly transformational neuro-plasticity in the people around you who love and respect you. Listen to that voice in your head that says, Steve needs you right now. Go, invite yourself over, and speak life into his situation.

Your role as a CEO is not to meet the ongoing primary needs of your people, but to have the greatest impact in the shortest amount of time and effort, like my mentor who came to visit at the right time, in the right way, being efficient and effective. Your role is to engage with impact and then refer. If you know how to access team and have a team that you can refer to, if you're just as happy to draw another circle around the situation and add another team member, then you will have the capacity to reach out to an infinite number of people. Connect and refer. Connect and refer. Do not get bogged down in your employees' process. This is not the role of a CEO.

What about when it is you who is on the couch, with a broken leg and broken thinking.?

When you're sick, sometimes you don't even know it. When you're broken, sometimes you don't even know it. When you're burnt out, sometimes you don't even know it. When you're switched off, sometimes you don't even know it. When you fade into Quadrant 1 and track into Quadrant 3, you often don't even know it.

BURNOUT

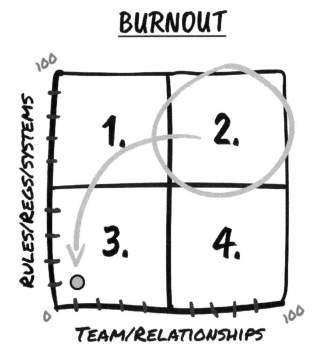

What about burnout?

Burnout is a combination of not enough team, systems that are not managing the volume and too much activity for a brain that is not managing historical, current and future worries and stress. Burnout happens slowly for most and unfortunately it can be disguised through the bad habits of the six profile coping methods. It's like being on a very long trek where you run out of energy. At this moment in your life you stand at a crossroad. The three choices are as follows.

1. The slow descent to the bottom of Quadrant 3, hypothermia. You end up curled up in a ditch getting really cold as the world passes you by. This is a passive, self-rejection cave-dwelling strategy.

2. The slow descent to the bottom of Quadrant 3, while throwing rocks at your friends. You become like a bull in a china shop. You revert to being that kid who has tears of rage coming out of their eyes whenever they're angry. You try to journey through life in red rage and that doesn't work, either. This is an aggressive, troll-like, snowball-throwing strategy.

3. The Switchback plan. You calm down, trust your friends, and let them strap you onto the stretcher and take you to the healer as you continue your descent into Quadrant 3.

Once, when I was speaking to a crowd of 750 about the importance of team, I handed out little orange and purple ribbons and an action step to the talk on TEAM. Orange ribbons signified that the person was able, willing and ready to pick up the corner of the stretcher for their friend right now. Purple ribbons were for folks who knew that to be healthy and functional right now they had to trust TEAM and get onto a stretcher and be carried for a season. I had the participants self-identify. At this moment in their lives, were they the person on the stretcher, or one of those buddies with strength, faith and capacity to pick up a corner of one of their friends' stretchers? We had about 400 ribbons of each color, and before we were even two-thirds of the way through the room we ran out of purple ribbons.

These were successful, well-dressed, urban people, and we saw in that moment that their big houses and fancy cars were not representative of the battles they were fighting in their thinking.

Often people assume positions of leadership insulate leaders from pain. As a CEO, you live in a tough world. It's not easy to maintain healthy functional TEAM around you. Somehow, you've got to find an inner circle that works. You have to build the capacity of TEAM around you, where you can be transparent and open.

Karen and I were in Paris in January, visiting our son and his family. They live just down the hill from one of Paris' attractions, the Sacré-cœur Basilica.

I was drawn to the church first as an attraction, and then at a much deeper level. Stepping into the space is fascinating. Hundreds of tourists are walking through the sanctuary while Catholic faithful are praying and making their confessions. I was struck by the absence of a sacrament like confession and prayer for most of us.

How can we practice being transparent and open? Sure, maybe we pay therapists, but it's not confession it's not prayer. They work in a very different modality.

It's time to build corporate cultures of peer support. I don't care if you find your peer support at work, in your family, or among your friends and community. What's important is having a small group of people whom you can trust with your Lane 3 challenges. It's time to build a peer support program where you know that every one of your senior leaders, all the way down to your supervisors, and your employees, are supported by their peers.

Here's the truth: As a CEO, through a 10-year career, you can spend 11 months on the stretcher, being carried by your peers, and do a world-class, Quadrant 2 job, if you have people willing to pick up the corners of that stretcher. If you don't, you're going toward either passivity or aggression, and you're going to make a mess of things.

There's nothing wrong with spending some stretcher time during a 10-year career. That's just normal humanity, it truly is. Imagine that you and your wife have a stillborn baby. You're on the stretcher! It's non-negotiable. Your life is great, and then you have a stillborn baby. The grief cycle begins. There is a healthy and a functional way to grieve, and there is an unhealthy dysfunctional way to process grief.

The Unhealthy, Dysfunctional Grief Process

Your wife takes the journey of active grief, she goes through all the cycles of grief. Your sociological commitment to the family is to keep on keeping on, to pay the bills and keep the lights on, so you go to work. You think you're making the right decision.

What you don't realize is that you've closed yourself out from team. Team happens in active grief, not the denial of grief. These things are non-negotiable. You have to take the journey of grief at some point. You can't skip these things. For the first 10 months you block out the grief, isolate from TEAM, close your door and work. When your brain catches the scent of your wife on the journey of healing from the stillborn baby, your brain takes you down into a delayed form of grief. It is misplaced, often misunderstood and very dangerous. There's proof of this if you look at the statistics of families where children have died of SIDS. There is a 70% divorce rate among these families. Delayed grief is very hard on relationships.

THE DELAYED GRIEF DECEPTION

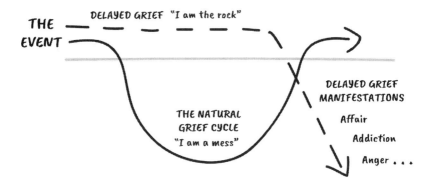

Delayed grief doesn't look like grief. This grief looks like an addiction. This grief looks like an affair. This grief looks like domestic violence. You get judged, and friends and relatives start talking, gossiping with disbelief about how your poor family's been through enough and this guy goes and has an affair with his secretary. How dare he, as CEO, pull that kind of stunt on his grieving family? This is all misplaced, however, and does not have to be your story.

Healthy, Functional Grief Process

Imagine the same story, though, where this time you're the CEO, and you and your wife are trying to get pregnant but it's been hard because you both have a lot of stress and it's complicated. It finally happens, your wife goes into the third trimester and she's 38 weeks and the baby stops moving. It's beyond trauma.

Now it all changes. You stop, breath, think, talk, act. And the act that you take is for your family, you, your wife, your 4 year old to get on a stretcher and with the help of your trusted friends with whom you've built capacity to continue the journey of life. You still go to work. The difference in this scenario is now you're not standing on your own two feet any more. You're being carried by your team. You and your wife and four-year-old son will be carried through this together, and it becomes a thing of beauty.

It becomes symbolic. You phone your friends, the ones carrying you on the stretcher, and tell them you're a mess but you still want to go to work. You ask for support through the process. Your buddy might ask what you mean by support. You might not know, but you're going to trust yourself and your buddies. You'll figure it out.

You go to work. You meet with your senior executives and say, "Here's the deal. I need to offload 30% of my responsibility." You ask them to share the load among them. You need to be home by 4 pm now, not 7 pm as it has been for years. You divvy up the tasks. You offer them your support in return, while hoping nothing like this ever happens to them. If it does, they have your word that you'll be picking up your corner of their stretcher.

Then you let the company know. You tell them you're coming to work but you're walking wounded. You ask them to cheer you on when you walk out of the building at 3:30 in the afternoon.

People want to help. People want to make a difference. Of course it's not ideal when your life has been pushed into Quadrant 3 with grief, pain and chaos; but if you've done your job, built capacity and strengthened your team, your life and career will stay afloat and people will rally in your support. The best thing is not to fake it. Your authenticity is what connects the team.

And when the light at the end of the tunnel of grief starts to shine for you and your family, you can journey towards the healing as a unit, in TEAM with the support of TEAM. At your retirement party, people will come to the mic and talk about these days as some of the most meaningful times they experienced in their lives. It's Quadrant 2. It's a world class culture.

Chapter 12

Aiming High

AN IMPORTANT PART OF HOW WE SET TARGETS AT Switchback is understanding that your brain is complex and can handle more than one fixed goal. Most organizations and CEOs have lost the art of aiming high. We're not saying set unrealistic goals, but we are suggesting that, to reach your targets, it may take aiming higher than the target.

Understandably, instead of setting targets that aim high, many CEOs have learned how to manage people's expectations. When somebody says, "You know what? You should aim way above what you plan to do," CEOs typically reply, "Yeah, you're talking to the wrong person here."

Of course, you can't go to your Board of Directors and tell them you're dreaming about doubling in size over the next two years because they'll reply that it makes no sense. Or they will hold you to it, which could be even worse. When you go to your Board of Directors and tell them it's realistic to have single-digit growth over the next 24 months and this is how you're going to achieve it, you've just given them a realistic and SMART (Specific, Measurable, Achievable, Relevant, Time-sensitive) goal.

Although SMART goals have become the go-to goal-setting map, they are not actually the best for your brain. Our brains actually benefit from conceptually overshooting the target, and that's not a SMART goal. Here's the truth: our brains are complex enough to have one part of the brain where you manage expectations and hit targets within decimal points, and at the same time establish what "aim high" category in another part of your brain lets you develop the thinking capacity to actually reach those targets.

Karen and I live on Vancouver Island on the west coast of Canada. On the protected side of Vancouver Island are 100s of small islands. Across from where we live are the Discovery Islands, the main one of which is Quadra. A little car and passenger ferry goes back and forth between Quadra and Vancouver Island, and docks in a cove on Quadra called Quathiaski Cove.

The water this little ferry traverses is called Discovery Passage, and at any time of the day the tidal waters can travel so fast that a yacht running at full steam against the tide can actually be traveling backwards. As a result of tidal action this section of the Pacific is one of the most alive oceans in the world; however, in this spot the water is quite treacherous. In fact, just north of Discovery Passage is Seymour Narrows, where the tides can run up to 15 knots with huge whirlpools and an infamous history of shipwrecks.

AIM HIGH

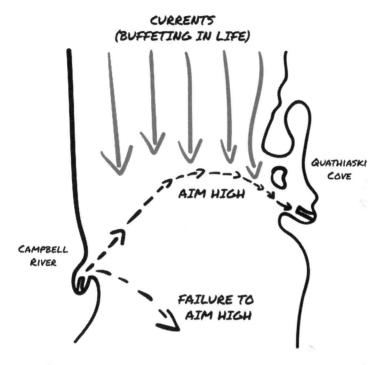

If the ferry captain pulls out of the Campbell River dock on our side of the water and aims for the dock at Quathiaski Cove, which is straight across this short passage, and the water is traveling at 8 knots, what's the likelihood of the ferry reaching that dock? Not very good. This is why the captain pulls out of Campbell River and aims the ferry, at full throttle, north of the target. The captain does this because the buffeting tidal current drives the ferry south and it takes an aim high strategy to land the ferry on target right at the dock in Quathiaski Cove.

This is how it goes in life. You're going to get pushed around a lot. Who hasn't been thrown off their course by the tidal currents of life? It's a human condition, and although you are a CEO, you are not exempt from this issue. Unfortunately, you are sometimes buffeted really hard. Sometimes it comes out of left field: family illness, one of your rock stars in the company gets headhunted and runs over to the competition, litigation, environmental crises, international trade blockades. Buffeting like this, those moments that leave you wondering what just went on, happen all the time.

Because buffeting can be expected, we need to have both SMART goals and aim-high goals operational at the same time. Your brain and your team can live in the tension of these two realities. The one reality is this: manage people's expectations, make SMART goals and don't exaggerate or overstate your opportunity. The other reality is to aim high and be ready because you know that your organization is up against very strong tidal currents and if you don't aim high you will not deliver. There's a lot of work for you to do as a CEO around building aim-high thinking within your leadership capacity and throughout your organization.

Building Trust

Building aim-high thinking within your organization depends a lot on the level of trust you have within your team. If you build enough mental toughness and maturity within your senior leadership team, even your board of directors, your team can hold in dynamic tension these two realities. They can figuratively aim for the moon while holding the whole organization to "realistic" targets.

Of course, what I love about Switchback is that not only is it vastly effective on the company level, it's also immediately transferable to our personal lives. Let's see how establishing targets, setting intentions, and aiming high all might play out in someone's personal life.

We once spent six days with a company, delivering two three-day trainings. In the second training, one of the leaders who had been part of both trainings came to the front of the room and explained that he had had a major breakthrough over the weekend. He was very excited to give the details. He explained to the room that he hated going to weddings. Why was that? It was because he often was seated at a table with strangers and was then stuck with them for over two hours, enduring a reception and speeches that he usually found boring and uncomfortable. From the Switchback training he decided for this particular wedding he would try the 3-Lane Highway tool (the communication tool we discussed in chapter 8) and see how it worked out. He also decided to aim high and set his targets way above any past experience: to connect at a Lane 3 level with everyone at the table while having his wife fall in love with him again.

He set his achievement and transformation intentions and set the target. He gamified something that was normally a horrible experience for him. All through the wedding, his wife couldn't figure out why he was in such a good mood. He told her it was because he had chosen to be. He was going to be a "switched-on" wedding guest. He knew how to integrate good material because he was a leader. He could do it quickly because he was bright and gifted.

This is the kind of situational awareness that so easily gets lost amid the forests of tight margins, or warrior cultures. For this leader, as he sat down at the table at the reception, he felt himself get excited, wondering what everyone's lives were like. He stopped, thought, and calmed himself down, and then started Lane 1 connections with the people at the table. He made easy conversation to begin, finding out where people were from, and their connection to the bride or groom. As he naturally paused, but kept the contact alive, people would give him opportunities to deepen the conversation with tickets.

All night, people kept talking, revealing their lives to him. His wife couldn't believe it was the same person. He told her, "People can change. I'm just working neuroplasticity." When he left the wedding, his brain was on fire. He had enjoyed such amazing connections with other humans he felt like he was alive again. Normally he would have been miserable, resentful towards his wife, filled with too much booze, and looking to pick a fight. This wedding marked a complete reversal for him. He hadn't really believed he could change his brain that fast and create a new outcome that quickly.

The work he really did was to set the achievement and transformational targets for improving his communication game. The night of the wedding, he set a clear intention to change how he approached what was formerly an unenjoyable time. Switchback gave him the thinking tools, but he had to choose to move the thinking into action. It starts with that choice.

It's all about an initial leap of faith and then the hard work of practice to build success. Believe that you can change, leverage TEAM, aim high, set your intentions, and then record, measure and analyze your progress.

How to Make It All Work

You know your company could do better. You know your leaders, managers, VPs could do better. You know a lot of people's home lives could be a lot better. You know the human impact and suffering that happens when people dissolve marriages and step outside of team, and how that impacts not only them personally, but their children and generations to come. You know all this. You're under a lot of pressure to perform bottom line metrics, and to do it all in a competitive workplace. You don't have a lot of time to do training. You don't even know how people are going to be able to manage what's coming down the pipe as it is. So how do you make Switchback work?

Number one, someone needs to be the sponsor. Guess who that person is? It's you. If you don't sponsor a program like Switchback, it will not move the needle of the culture. While you'll end up with departmental change, you won't have company-wide change.

At the end of the day, the big target is long-term, sustainable, cultural transformation. For that to happen, the sponsorship needs to come from the top. Better to take your time and step through a process than to do a momentary campaign. Campaigns are pretty interesting and fun, but they're like peacocks: the feathers come out, it's really exciting, and then everyone wonders what will happen next. And if nothing does happen next, there's a tendency for people to go back to their old pathways.

Second, a champion needs to come forward. Somebody within your organization has to be the champion. The higher up the organizational chart, the better. The higher respected, the better. A Quadrant 2 champion will build out a world class project management plan while building excitement, anticipation and expectation. It doesn't have to be your Safety or HR leader. We have run very successful programs with Corporate Services VPs or Operational VPs as the champions.

An anthropologist named Anthony Wallace wrote an article in 1956 about "Revitalization Movements." Wallace proposed a model that he claimed was transcultural, and that applied to small nations experiencing coups, to companies having struggles, and to families in societies and tribes. He basically said that there are two primary components to running a successful revitalization movement. The first is a "no apologies messianic call to action", a statement around belief, not process, and the second is a logical, sequential, step-by-step process to meet the goal.

We can look at the Canadian west coast logging industry to find an example of an Anthony Wallace Revitalization Movement. This industry historically had a high rate of accidental death, and it had to change. The unapologetic messianic statement was:

"Everyone comes home safe every day, and we are going to build an industry-wide team that cares and supports each other, combined with new rules, regulations, systems, certifications and audits."

It was the perfect Quadrant 2 plan. The companies that have followed this call to action and system have seen tremendous results.

The higher that message and the messenger within the organization, the more effective the outcome. In truth, you are the best messenger for the messianic statement. That was the old way; this is the new way. We need to stop doing that; we need to start doing this.

The logical, sequential, step-by-step process to reach the messianic goal is what Wallace called the journey to the "new steady state." This is basic project management, and most of your company will have really high levels of expertise in this area. What they haven't done, though, is apply project management theory to human complexity. For your culture shift to be successful, you'll need a strong, passionate statement. "This is where we're heading, and this is where I believe we can go. Here's the target: we're going to aim high".

A statement like this actually creates short-term stress. The organization will have anxiety around the future. This stress and anxiety is resolved with clarity about how to: execute, audit, hold people accountable, measure, reward and celebrate. When that takes place, the old way becomes unattractive, and there's a sense of hope (because of the messianic statement) and a sense of possibility because now the path to the new way can be seen. Most people will be inspired by the target, understand the plan and adopt the change. There will be late adopters and resistors (remember the six profiles). That's not a problem. That's just normal. Just be sure that the late adopters and resistors actually do eventually adopt.

Once you have people essentially on the new path, your next goal is to make it sustainable. Your new model has to deliver less day-to-day and chronic stress to the individual, to the team, to the department, to the corporation, to the client, and to the asset, than was occurring using the old way. If the new way delivers more stress, more worry, or more anxiety, people will abandon the new way and go back to the old path.

How long does it take to shift the culture? We've all seen that a negative culture shift can happen quickly, and I believe a positive culture shift can also happen quickly. Where most of the companies I work with have gotten stuck is around how to best sustain the change to a positive culture.

Using the Anthony Wallace model, you can execute a very quick cultural transformation that's backed up by operational excellence. If it has a sustained reduction of stress, and an increase in resilience, happiness and productivity, then you have achieved a revitalization movement.

When people who study culture-change say it takes seven to eight years to shift a culture, I have a hunch that what they've observed are multiple attempts and multiple failures. I myself have witnessed, first-hand, gifted CEOs set a new course for their companies, back it up with really great systems and structures, hold people accountable to it, measure it, audit it, and successfully pull it off in a fraction of the industry-standard time frame.

Switchback brings to the table the ability to accomplish this with the human factor at the forefront. It's the missing piece in your otherwise world-class structure. The digital age has created this incredible ability to make our systems robust with cloud technology and all the rest. We need to apply that same level of intensity to the human component of our business models. We think Switchback offers the perfect combination of live training, digital tracking, cloud-based analysis, e-learning, personal growth, and turnkey peer support programs to do just that.

Imagine it's six months from now, and your company has partnered with Switchback. We are embedded, dearly loved and respected at all levels of your company after your team engaged with our live training, which is entertaining, challenging and aligned to your culture. The Switchback Feedback App is collecting weekly pulse surveys and help you understand at a grass roots level the needs of your employees and departments. You have employees who are engaged online, sitting with their families, watching Switchback TV, learning together and sorting out their issues.

You've introduced your employees' families to a system that is transforming their lives. Will an employee so transformed steal from you in any way, be it time, effort, thoughts, or even actual physical products? Not on your life. Will that employee be looking over the fence and wanting to be recruited by somebody else? Not likely. Will that employee have a healthy, functional view of identity around work and life balance? Yes. Is that to your advantage? Of course it is, in the long term. Will that employee potentially be able to move beyond their current status and overcome the barriers of advancement, so they can go from being operational to supervisory to management to senior management, and even reengage in the academic process? Is it to the benefit of your company to have your workforce graduating themselves up to the next levels?

I have a hunch that human capital is going to be one of the most valued pieces of the puzzle moving forward, as I believe there will be huge employment opportunities within companies. We will see companies with legitimate markets and legitimate products, but without the people to execute the process. Imagine if you're leading the company that stands apart from your competitors because you paid attention to the people, and you built capacity and there was a natural progression within. Think about the bench strength that your company would have, and the innovation that would come through the system.

A lot of companies are trying to get their grassroots workers to report near misses at the safety level because it's been found that most employees or contractors are very reluctant to report a near miss or a close call. They report the ones that are obvious, like the truck in the ditch or the belt completely off the pulley, the incidents they know they have to report. It is the things that happen where they don't think anyone saw them do it that are being buried. They're buried because corporate culture has in general shifted into Quadrant 1 on a good day and Quadrant 3 on a bad day. We have these great programs, including drug and alcohol programs, but if they are delivered through Quadrant 1 high rules, low relationship culture, these very solid programs grossly under-perform. Foundationally get your company culture into Quadrant 2 and then watch as your systems outperform your expectations.

Realistically, if the process is Quadrant 1, and it only has a punitive, authoritative model attached to it, why would a contractor jeopardize their livelihood to meet your standard of reporting? All your policies and procedures need to be tested and tried through the 4 Quadrant, front-of-the-brain matrix.

Within a union environment, there's absolutely nothing wrong with a clearly laid out collective agreement regarding progressive discipline, but progressive discipline is actually your second choice. The first choice is to coach to compliance, because that's what shows interest in human complexity. Learn from experiences. If somebody does something that is a gross infraction and breaks the union agreement, no problem. Apply progressive discipline but continue to ask the why questions. Why did she do that? What was her motivation? Take a step back, use the gap, exercise 3-Lane communication, take a moment and ask the right questions, so that everyone can learn from these experiences.

If, at the end of learning you conclude that this person is malicious, rebellious, and essentially non-repentant, then, of course, exercise your right within the collective agreement to go through progressive discipline. But if the person made an honest mistake because they had a moment of back brain reactivity and lost their focus, and they were able to identify why and then process it with their family and colleagues and seek out professional help, and if this made a difference in their life, then you have just renovated a human being.

If this kind of care and attention – which is actually less work than progressive discipline – is successful, what does this do for loyalty and trust within your team? What is that employee doing when she talks to her friends and colleagues on the weekend about the company that she works for? She'll be telling them about how she made an honest mistake, and her company would have been fully justified to terminate her because of it, but they took an alternative route.

She'll talk with her friends about how the company took the time to listen, dug deeper into her life, and offered resources to help her. She'll tell her friends about how she found a group to go to, an online community for support, and books to read. At the end, she might even tell her friends she no longer feels like the same person, and that she credits her supervisor and manager at her workplace for this change in her life.

This is a brand that you can be proud of. It's safer, faster, quicker, nimbler, more innovative, and world-class. It's also completely human. This is how Switchback

193

has crossed cultural barriers and works on the global level. This is how Switchback is effective: it's about making choices that take every individual's basic humanity into account.

At the end of the day, we thank you for taking the leadership burden of being a CEO. It's huge, and it's not easy. It's complex and challenging to its core. We believe that if you follow the principles as well as the targets and guidelines of Switchback, you can stand at the crossroads and choose to be a Switched-On CEO with a world class culture.

If tragedy does hit your company, which I hope it never does, you will have the capacity and the ability to walk through the front door of the grieving family and represent the best that leadership can be. In that moment, you can be the face and the hands of care and compassion. You will know that you are choosing a human path, you are choosing the right way. Even though a lot of people would say that to stand with a grieving family after an industrial fatality is one of the most difficult things about being a CEO, you will actually have rest for your soul, because you know that you have aligned your company with principles and values that give you the best chance at having this not take place on your watch.

Do bad things happen to good people? Absolutely. Is Switchback foolproof? Absolutely not. But we are confident in our position that Switchback is one of the most powerful human factor tools that you can implement within the culture of your organization to actually see the culture dial move.

On behalf of Switchback and those who have engaged in this transformational process, we wish you great success moving forward.

Conclusion

As a re-cap, why set your intentions on being a Switched-on CEO? Because your brain was designed to function at this level, your team needs you at this level and your family is hoping that you will connect with them at this level.

Please do this one thing: rethink your current beliefs about people's ability to change, and the power of team. At Switchback, we know that people can change, and the power of success is in team. You can solve your complex culture issues with speed and efficiency. How? By reaching out to team that you can trust to deliver the transformation. My personal and professional calling is to build a brand-new opportunity for you and your most challenging people. We have built a team that travels the world implementing this transformational power.

I hope that now you're eager to connect with us. There are several options to help you get started. Our team is committed to working with organizations just like yours and helping them achieve the goals they're striving for. You can see for yourself how robust the Switchback model is.

One way to get started is to call us and invite us over. We also have Switchback TV, an e-learning platform, as another entry point into Switchback and one you can introduce to your team. The e-learning platform is all modular video learning. It's documented and gamified for your employees and, more importantly, it's for you personally.

We're very committed to psychometrics and we've built a model, based on Switchback, that lets you track the culture of your company and get real-life feedback on a weekly basis. It only takes a touch screen and about five seconds for an employee to record their thoughts about their own health and functionality, and the state of their team and the company culture as a whole. From that, you get complex, robust, deep data that translates into PowerPoint presentation-style slides for you, your executive and your Board of Directors.

While we hope you enjoyed the journey this book has taken you on, keep in mind that no journey is complete until you actually do something. If you're like most CEOs, we know you are great at motivating and helping others. After all you got the job because of your competence and leadership skills. However, consider this saying: "The higher you climb the lonelier it gets." Remember the second fundamental belief of Switchback: the power of success is in team.

Keeping this in mind, here is our top recommendation for action you can take today on your Switchback journey: build stronger team around you, for your own sake. Surround yourself with people you can trust. People you can talk about your Xs with. People who will travel into Lane 3 with you. People who can help you when you start heading towards the bottom of Quadrant 3.

Never underestimate the value of team in your life; I had a gifted brother-in-law who took his life in 2016. As I continue to grieve his death and think about why, it is clear that a lack of real honest team around him is at the top of the list.

Life is hard; life is beautiful. Either way, it is better in team. You don't need 35 new best friends; just a couple. How can you build your team, beginning today? Start with the obvious:

1. Your spouse is potentially your greatest teammate. Our partners are literally three inches from us on any given night. They are so close and yet at the same time can feel like a million miles away. Consider reaching out using the tools described in these pages.

2. Your children. As adults, your children can become fantastic friends if you are willing to trust them with your Xs. It's the oldest trick in the book. Do you want your adult children to open up to you? Open up first before you ask the same of them. Welcome, you say. (Lane 1) I'm so glad you guys can join us for dinner (Lane 2). I had a super hard meeting today. It is still renting space in my brain (Lane 3). How was your battleground today (Lane 3)? Now they can go two ways: help you unpack your day or start to unpack their day. Either way, world-class team.

3. Your long-term friends who have shifted into Logging Road buddies or at best Lane 2 communicators. With a bit of work and setting of intentions some of

them can merge back into healthy, functional relationship and join you on the 3 Lane Highway.

4. Professionals: coaches, pastors, counselors: someone in these fields might be a fit who encourages the level of honesty in you that you know is needed.

5. Treasure hunt: Set your intentions on developing a couple of new contacts for the purpose of peer support. Now engage your peripheral vision and watch for them. Test every potential new relationship with your internal integrity grid.

6. Pay the money and join a Mastermind Group. These groups collect people with similar leadership responsibilities and intentionally build trust, openness and honesty for a variety of reasons. We have a Mastermind Group, if you are interested.

I started the book with the thought that probably 90% of your life is good, and that Switchback can help transform the 10% that has the potential to sabotage your success. The offer still holds. It is amazing when successful people are able and willing to reach out to TEAM and gain even more resilience to serve this beautiful world we share.

7. Most of all, remember the fundamental beliefs:

People Can Change
and
The Power of Success is in TEAM.

We are here to support and encourage you as you transform your life, your work culture and your home.

Be a Switched-on CEO.
Think like a World Class Leader.

Don't delay.
Reach out right now.

It's your move...

With my greatest respect

Steven Falk MA
Founder / CEO
Switchback Systems Corp

Your friend who has been transformed by avoidable workplace fatalities, and the impacted families, co-workers and CEOs who pick up the phone and asked for TEAM.

Acknowledgements

To the CEOs around the world who have opened their lives up to Switchback and given us their insights into the complexity of leadership.

To the many clients over the past three decades who have challenged my thinking through their pain, sorrow, breakthroughs and successes. You took a chance on team and together we created pathways of hope.

To the dedicated Switchback team. Your courage and strength, vision and wisdom are making a difference in the lives of hundreds of leaders in government, business and organizations. I sleep better at night knowing you are world class ambassadors of our cause.

To my family clan. Not everyone has the blessing of being part of a large clan. You all inspire and ground me. May my ceiling be the floor of the next generations to come.

About the Author

STEVEN R. FALK is the CEO and Founder of Switchback Systems Corp (2009), a Canadian full- service consulting / digital metrics company with a global client base. Prior to Switchback, Steven owned and operated a successful Marriage and Family Therapy private practice for 22 years. He holds Bachelor of Arts and Master of Arts degrees.

Steven gained international recognition through his work in the natural resource sector helping reduce fatality and injury rates in high human exposure environments. Steven is in demand as a keynote speaker at regional and national conferences and focuses his presentations on how to leverage the human brain to revitalize teams and organizational cultures. Steven's ability to take complex issues and transform them into profound but simple-to-understand diagrams is what sets him apart in the industry. This externalization and understanding of inner thoughts and team dynamics is the difference-maker for many organizations around the world. Recently, Switchback Systems Corp has produced new culture-tracking software so organizations can better understand, measure and report the complexity of human thinking, teams and organizational culture.

Steven lives on Vancouver Island with his wife Karen. Their four children are happily building the next generation with the count currently at seven.

39237894R00124

Made in the USA
Columbia, SC
09 December 2018